Go Fish, SNOOPY!

by Charles M. Schulz

Selected Cartoons from
I'M NOT YOUR SWEET BABBOO!
Volume 1

FAWCETT CREST • NEW YORK

A Fawcett Crest Book
Published by Ballantine Books
Contents of Book: PEANUTS® Comic Strips by Charles M. Schulz
                    Copyright © 1983 by United Feature Syndicate, Inc.

Library of Congress Catalog Card Number: 84-80690

ISBN 0-449-20787-0

This book comprises a portion of I'M NOT YOUR SWEET BABBOO! and is
reprinted by arrangement with Hold, Rinehart and Winston

Printed in Canada

First Ballantine Books Edition: October 1985

10 9 8 7 6 5 4 3 2 1

Go Fish, SNOOPY!

SMAK

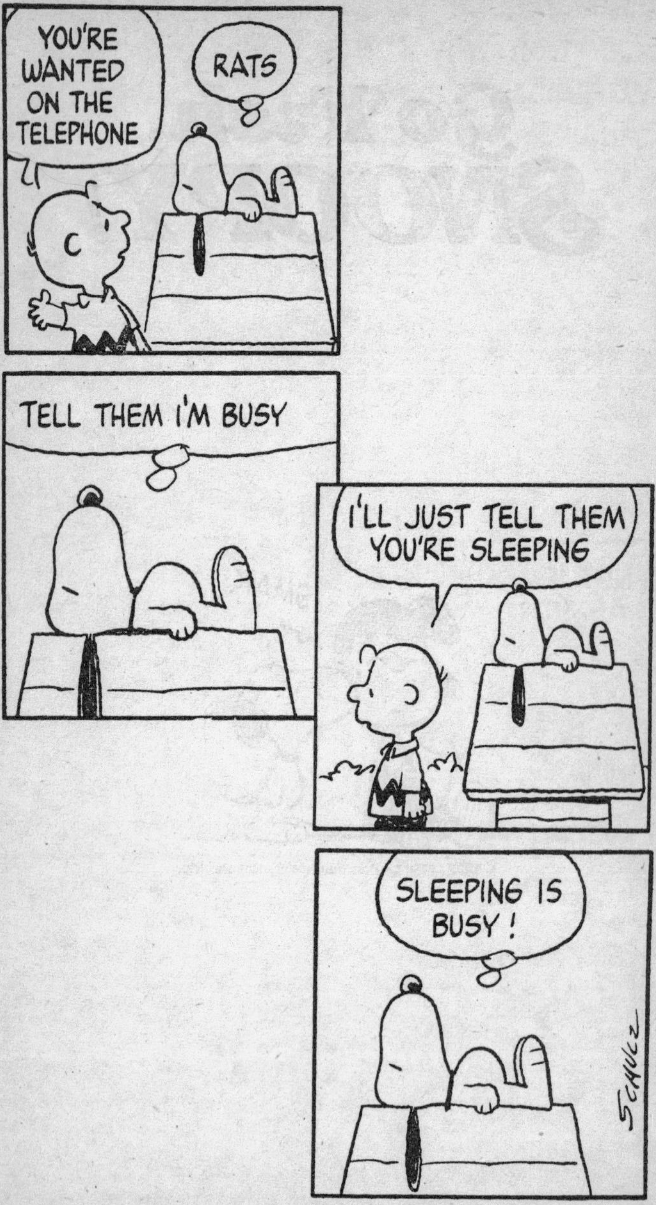
YOU'RE WANTED ON THE TELEPHONE
RATS
TELL THEM I'M BUSY
I'LL JUST TELL THEM YOU'RE SLEEPING
SLEEPING IS BUSY!
SCHULZ

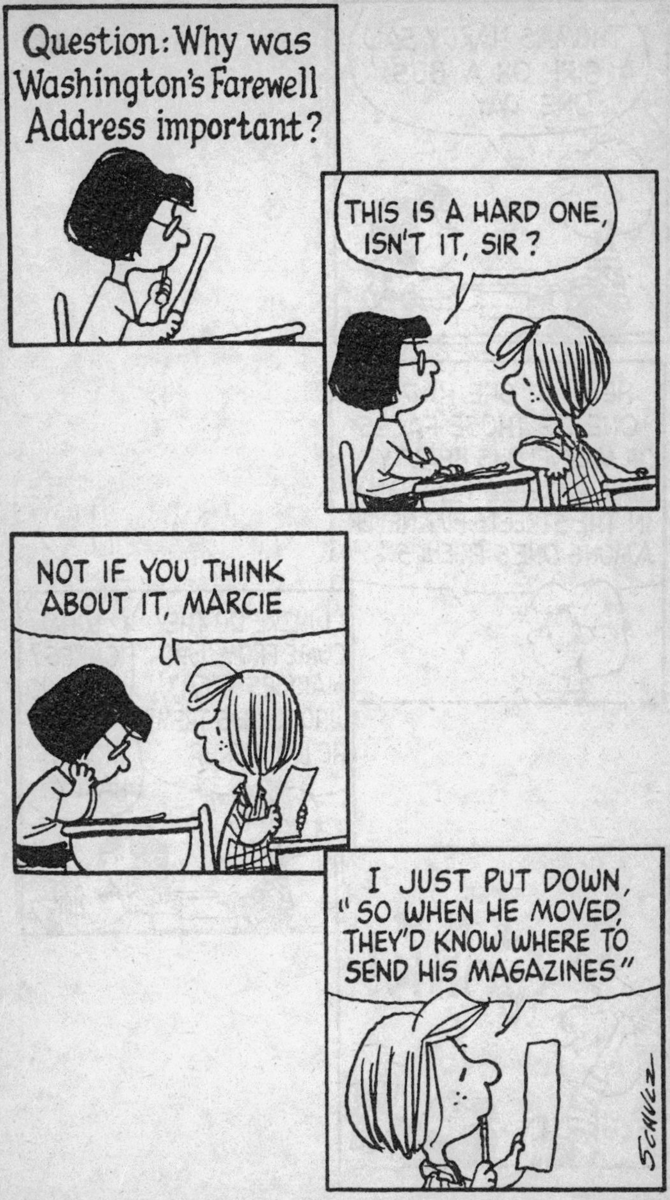
Question: Why was Washington's Farewell Address important?
THIS IS A HARD ONE, ISN'T IT, SIR?
NOT IF YOU THINK ABOUT IT, MARCIE
I JUST PUT DOWN, "SO WHEN HE MOVED, THEY'D KNOW WHERE TO SEND HIS MAGAZINES"
SCHULZ

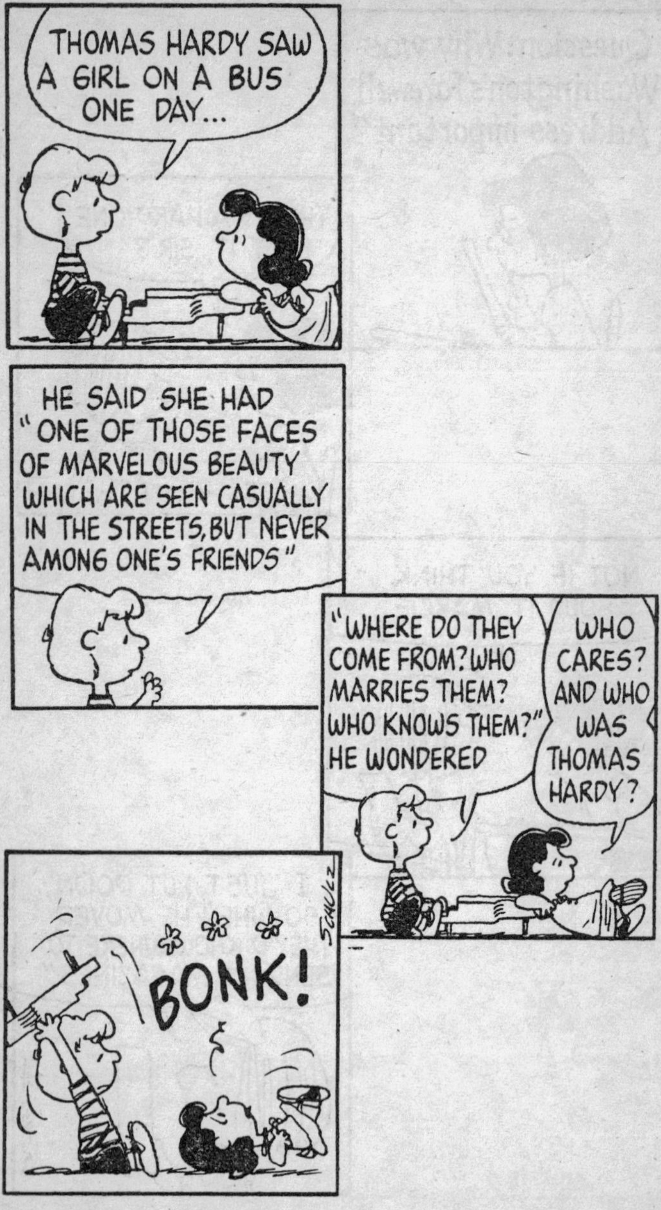
THOMAS HARDY SAW A GIRL ON A BUS ONE DAY...
HE SAID SHE HAD "ONE OF THOSE FACES OF MARVELOUS BEAUTY WHICH ARE SEEN CASUALLY IN THE STREETS, BUT NEVER AMONG ONE'S FRIENDS"
"WHERE DO THEY COME FROM? WHO MARRIES THEM? WHO KNOWS THEM?" HE WONDERED
WHO CARES? AND WHO WAS THOMAS HARDY?
BONK!
SCHULZ

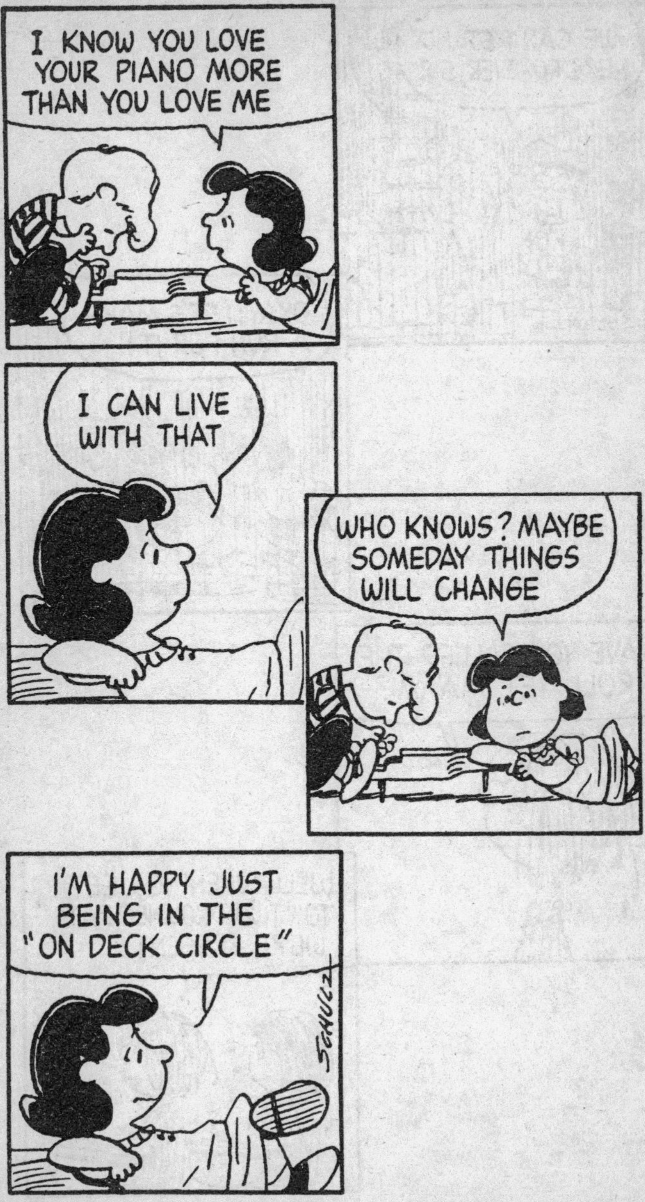
I KNOW YOU LOVE YOUR PIANO MORE THAN YOU LOVE ME
I CAN LIVE WITH THAT
WHO KNOWS? MAYBE SOMEDAY THINGS WILL CHANGE
I'M HAPPY JUST BEING IN THE "ON DECK CIRCLE"
SCHULZ

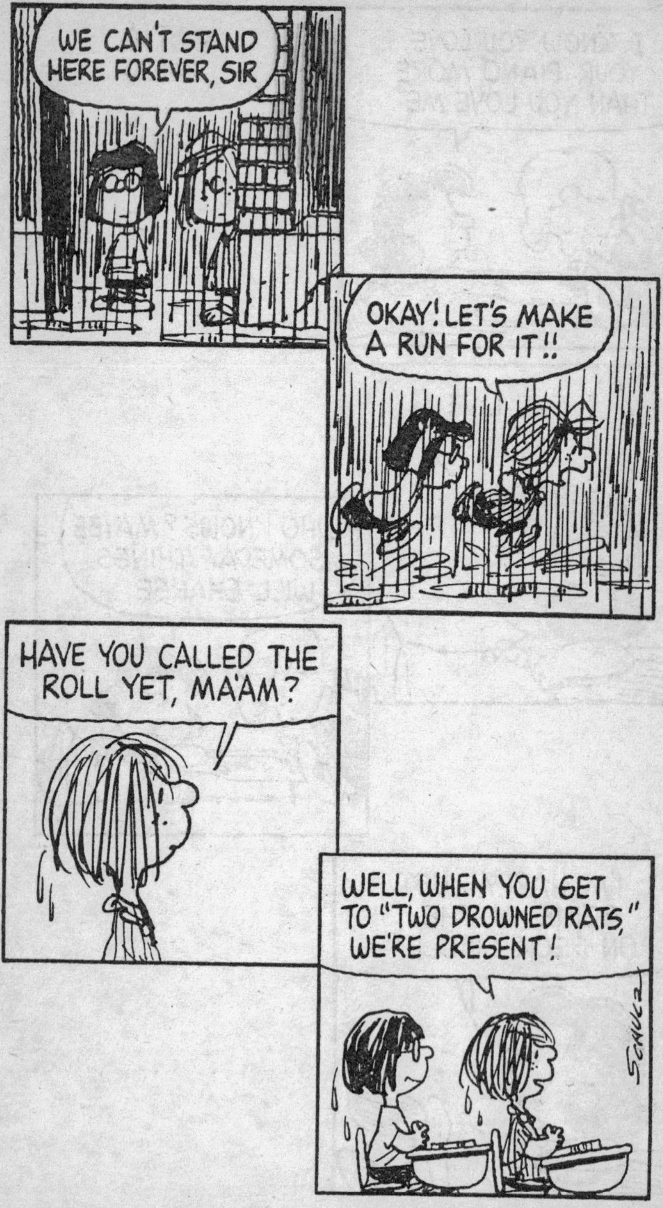
WE CAN'T STAND HERE FOREVER, SIR
OKAY! LET'S MAKE A RUN FOR IT!!
HAVE YOU CALLED THE ROLL YET, MA'AM?
WELL, WHEN YOU GET TO "TWO DROWNED RATS," WE'RE PRESENT!
SCHULZ

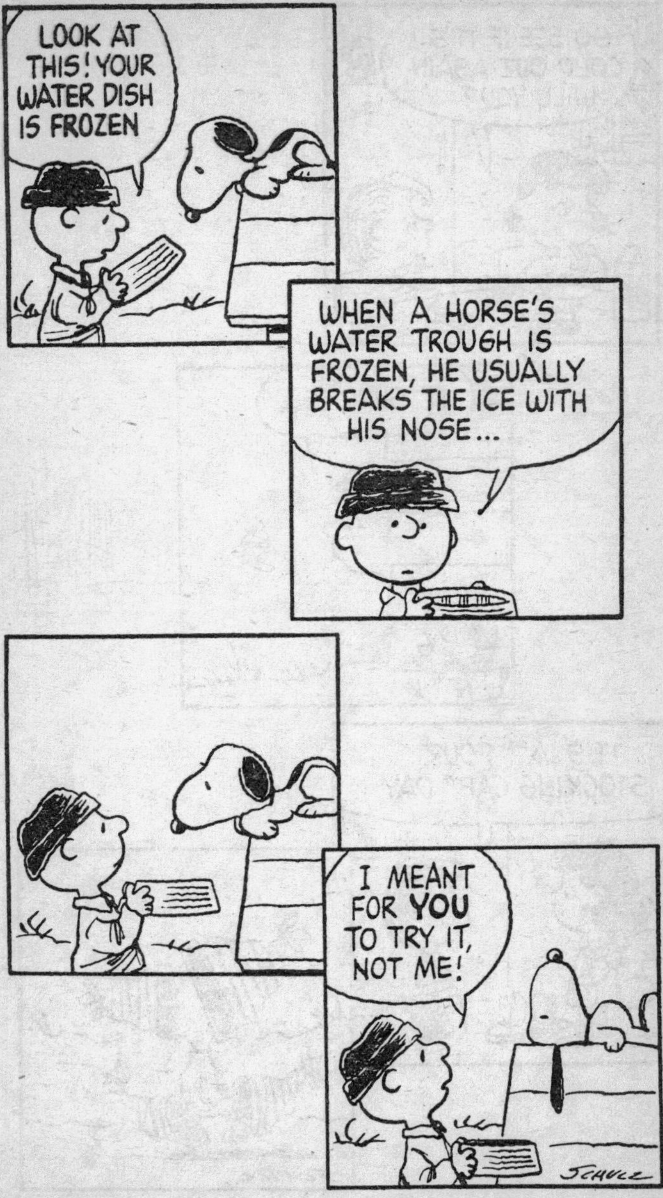
LOOK AT THIS! YOUR WATER DISH IS FROZEN
WHEN A HORSE'S WATER TROUGH IS FROZEN, HE USUALLY BREAKS THE ICE WITH HIS NOSE...
I MEANT FOR **YOU** TO TRY IT, NOT ME!
SCHULZ

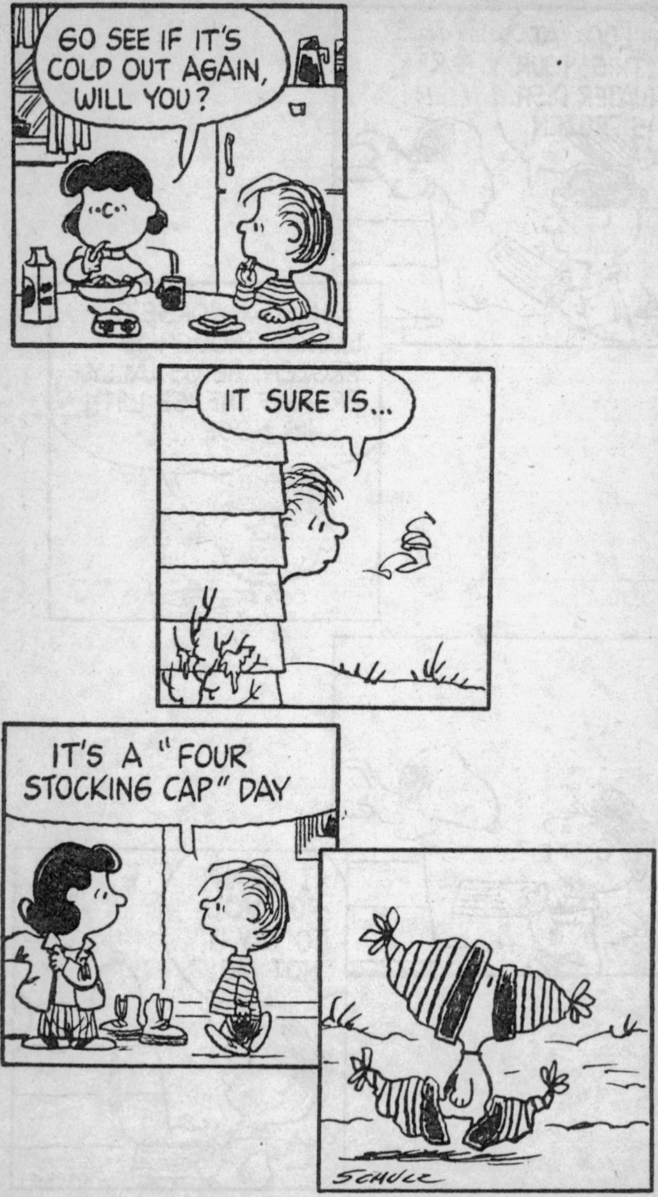
GO SEE IF IT'S COLD OUT AGAIN, WILL YOU?
IT SURE IS...
IT'S A "FOUR STOCKING CAP" DAY
SCHULZ

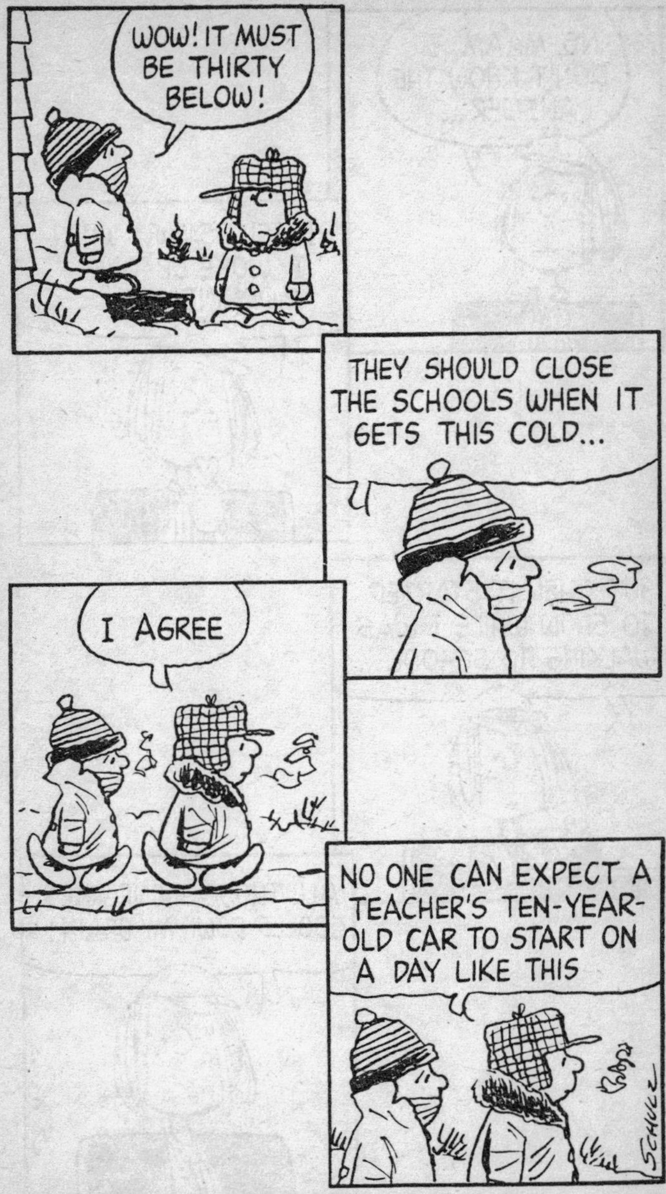
WOW! IT MUST BE THIRTY BELOW!
THEY SHOULD CLOSE THE SCHOOLS WHEN IT GETS THIS COLD...
I AGREE
NO ONE CAN EXPECT A TEACHER'S TEN-YEAR-OLD CAR TO START ON A DAY LIKE THIS
SCHULZ

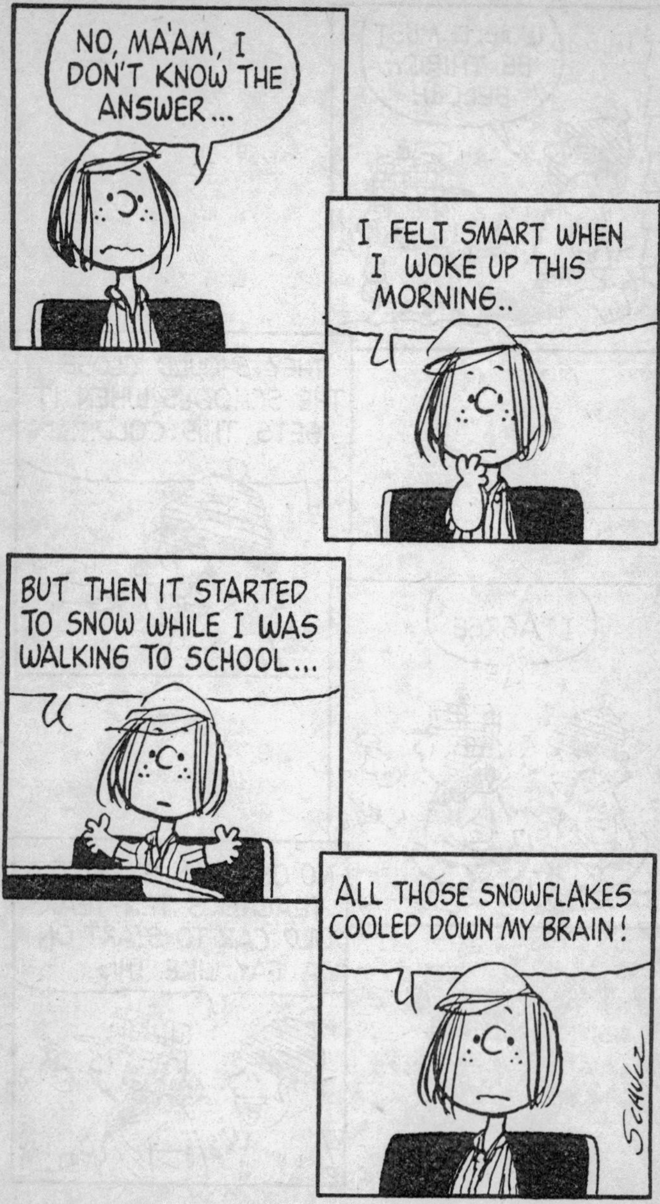
NO, MA'AM, I DON'T KNOW THE ANSWER...
I FELT SMART WHEN I WOKE UP THIS MORNING..
BUT THEN IT STARTED TO SNOW WHILE I WAS WALKING TO SCHOOL...
ALL THOSE SNOWFLAKES COOLED DOWN MY BRAIN!
SCHULZ

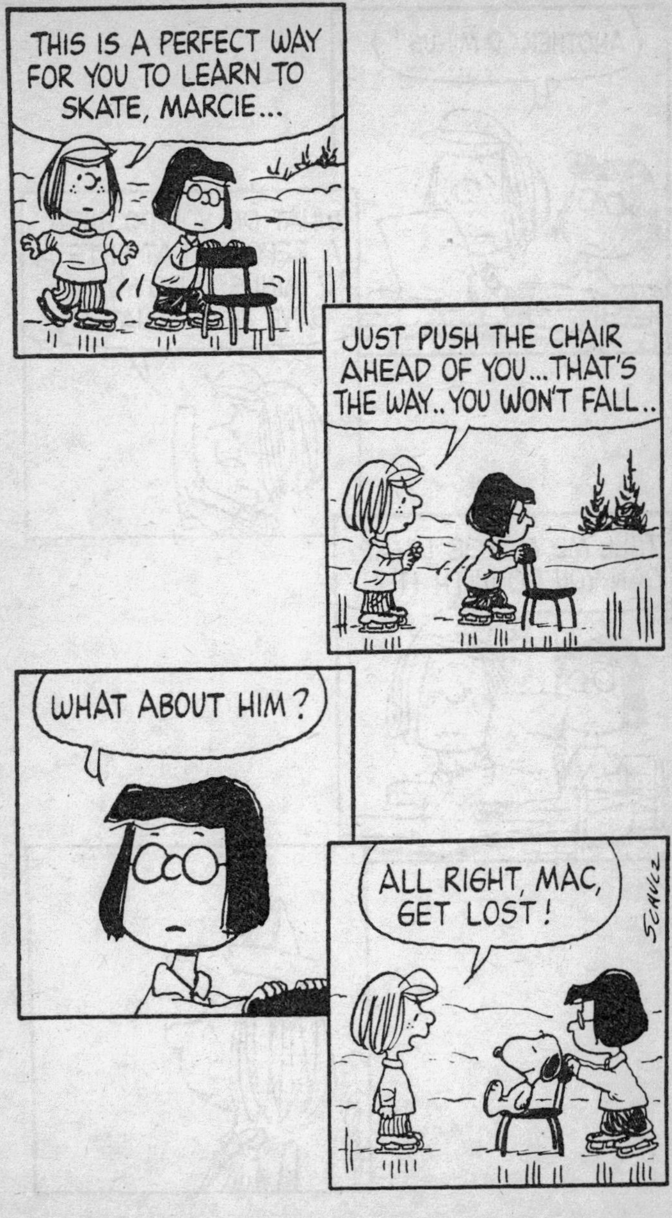
THIS IS A PERFECT WAY FOR YOU TO LEARN TO SKATE, MARCIE...
JUST PUSH THE CHAIR AHEAD OF YOU...THAT'S THE WAY.. YOU WON'T FALL..
WHAT ABOUT HIM?
ALL RIGHT, MAC, GET LOST!
SCHULZ

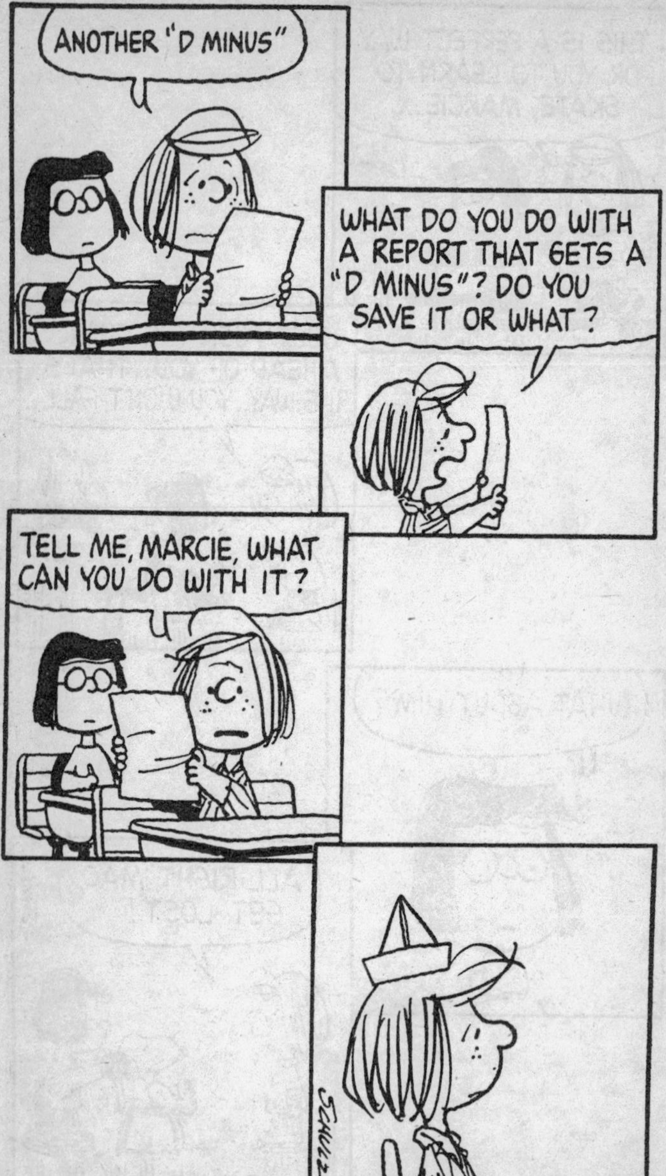
ANOTHER "D MINUS"
WHAT DO YOU DO WITH A REPORT THAT GETS A "D MINUS"? DO YOU SAVE IT OR WHAT?
TELL ME, MARCIE, WHAT CAN YOU DO WITH IT?
SCHULZ

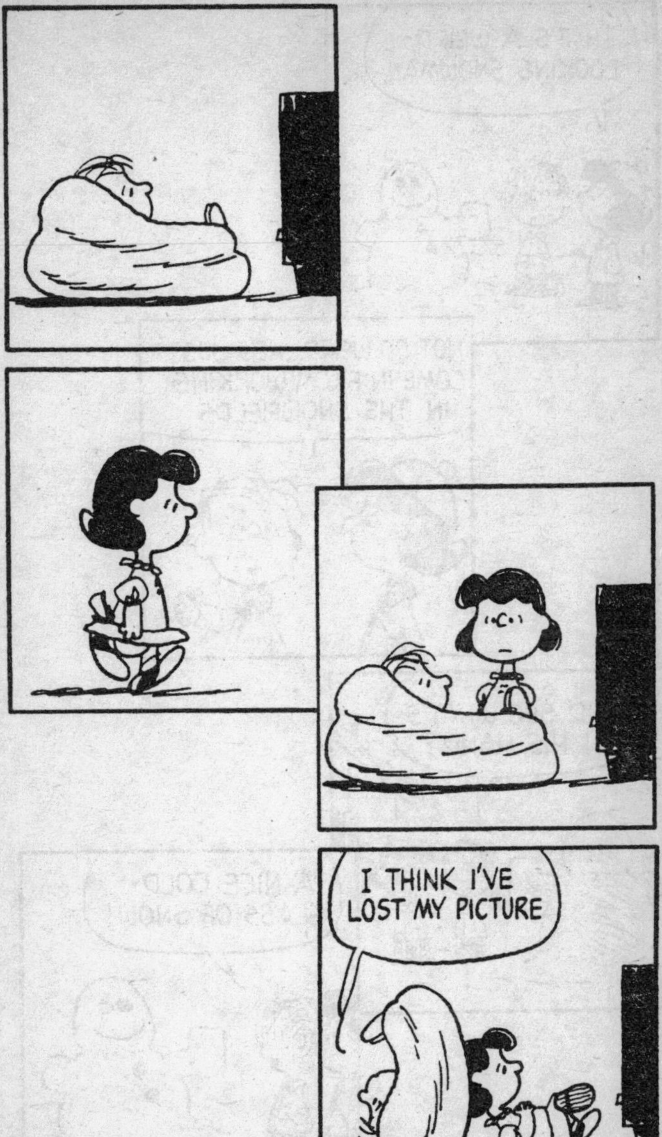
I THINK I'VE LOST MY PICTURE
SCHULZ

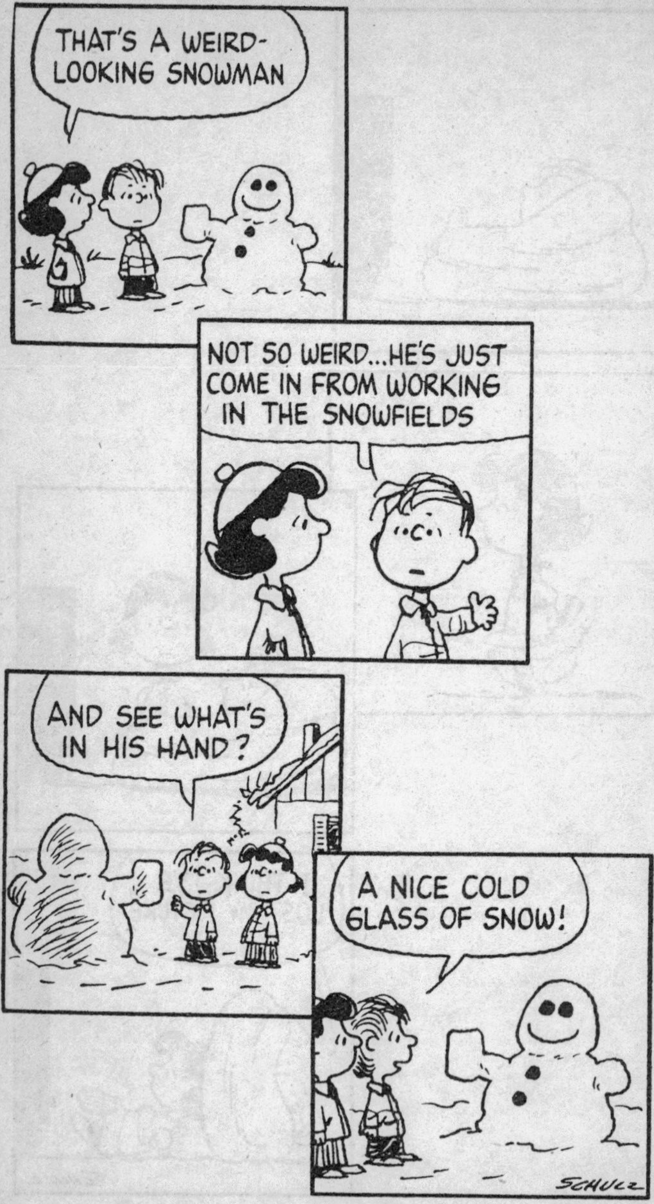
THAT'S A WEIRD-LOOKING SNOWMAN
NOT SO WEIRD...HE'S JUST COME IN FROM WORKING IN THE SNOWFIELDS
AND SEE WHAT'S IN HIS HAND?
A NICE COLD GLASS OF SNOW!
SCHULZ

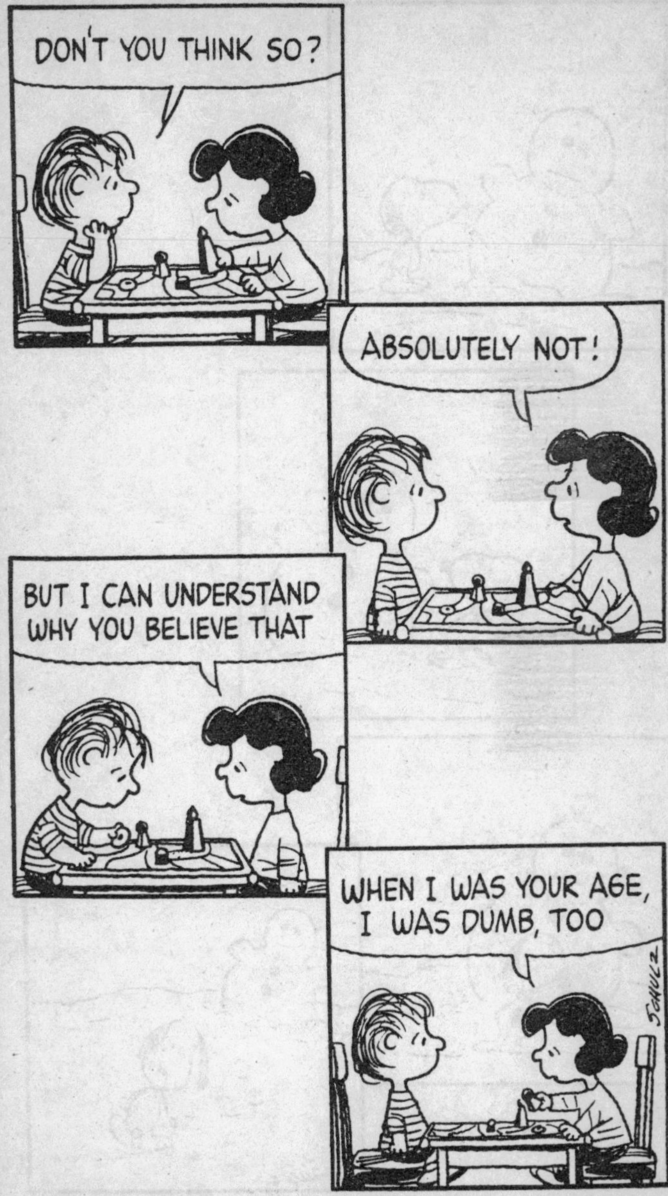
DON'T YOU THINK SO?
ABSOLUTELY NOT!
BUT I CAN UNDERSTAND WHY YOU BELIEVE THAT
WHEN I WAS YOUR AGE, I WAS DUMB, TOO

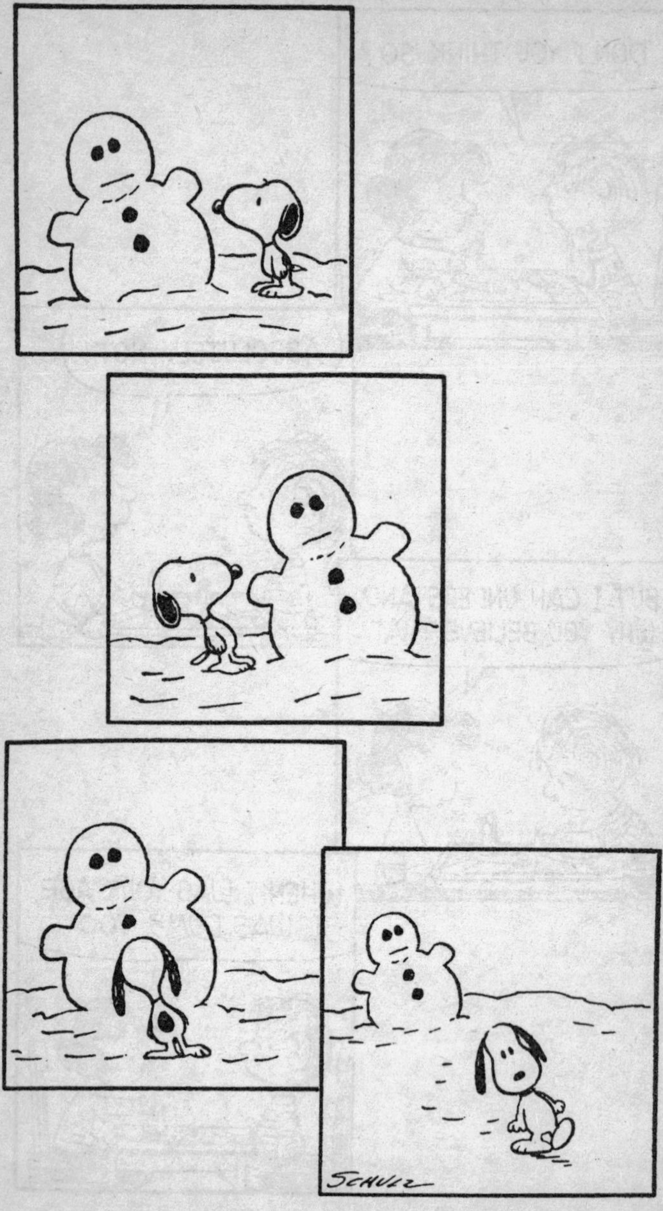
SCHULZ

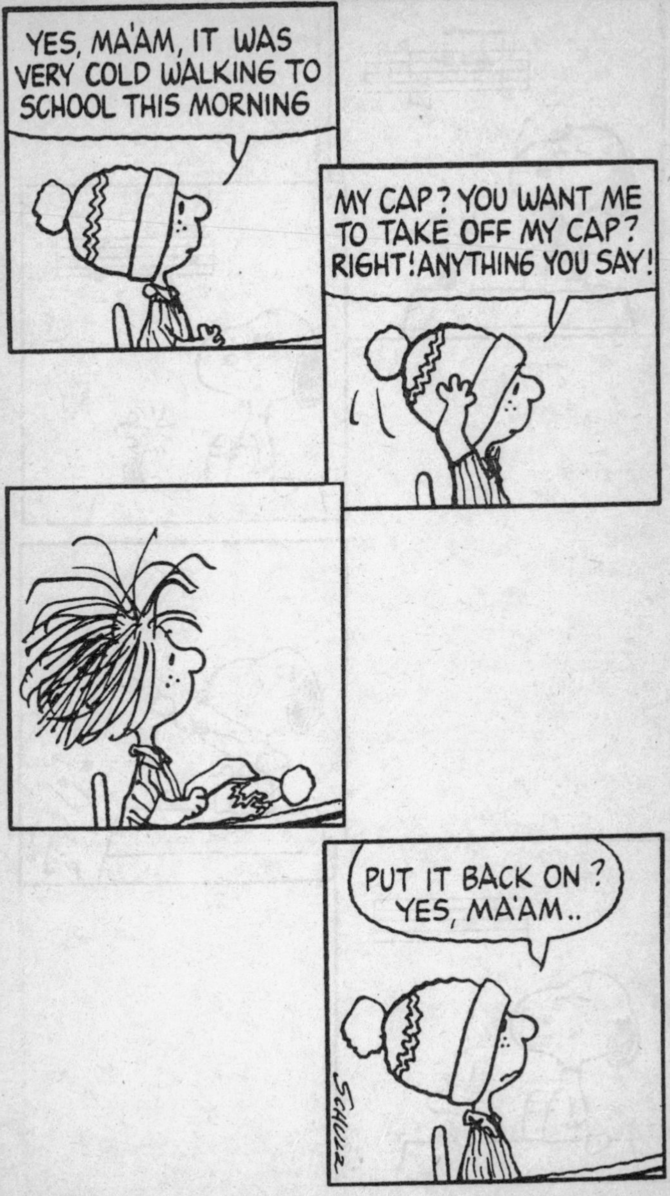
YES, MA'AM, IT WAS VERY COLD WALKING TO SCHOOL THIS MORNING
MY CAP? YOU WANT ME TO TAKE OFF MY CAP? RIGHT! ANYTHING YOU SAY!
PUT IT BACK ON? YES, MA'AM..
SCHULZ

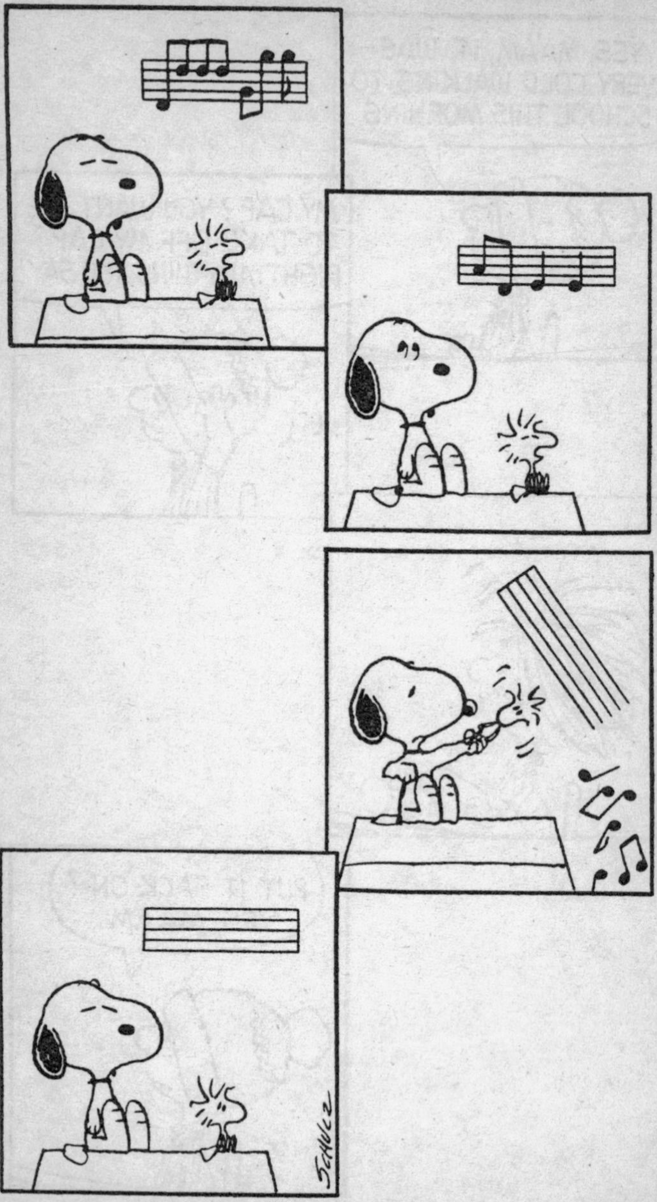
SCHULZ

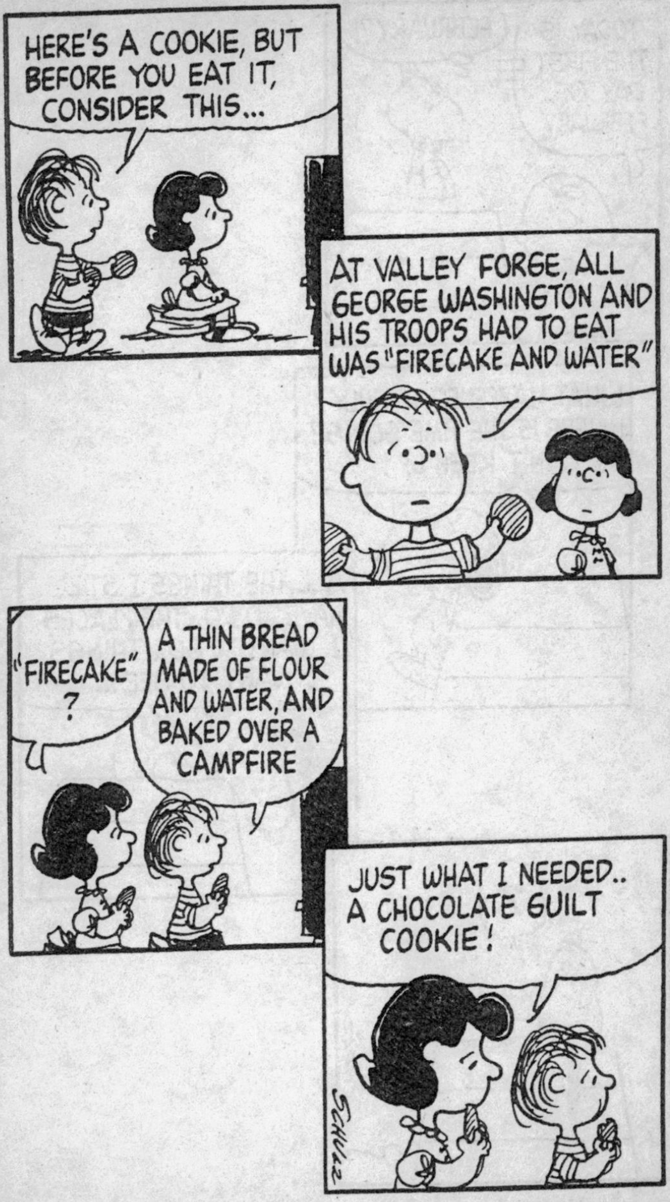
HERE'S A COOKIE, BUT BEFORE YOU EAT IT, CONSIDER THIS...
AT VALLEY FORGE, ALL GEORGE WASHINGTON AND HIS TROOPS HAD TO EAT WAS "FIRECAKE AND WATER"
"FIRECAKE" ?
A THIN BREAD MADE OF FLOUR AND WATER, AND BAKED OVER A CAMPFIRE
JUST WHAT I NEEDED.. A CHOCOLATE GUILT COOKIE !
SCHULZ

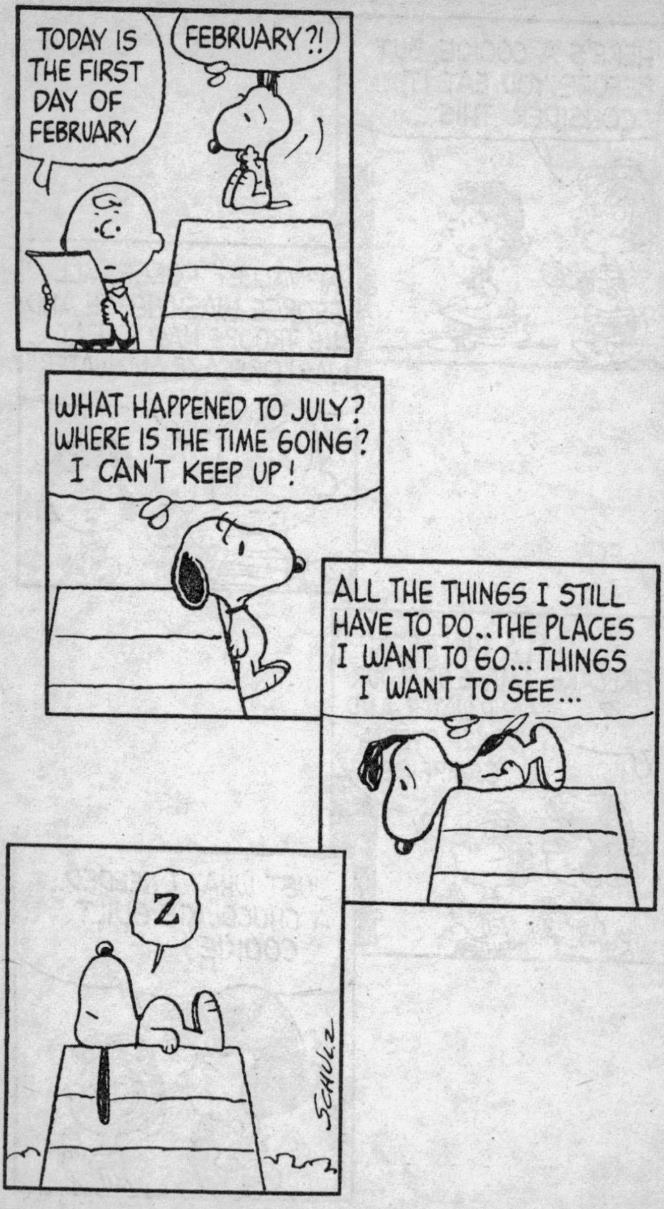
TODAY IS THE FIRST DAY OF FEBRUARY
FEBRUARY?!
WHAT HAPPENED TO JULY? WHERE IS THE TIME GOING? I CAN'T KEEP UP!
ALL THE THINGS I STILL HAVE TO DO..THE PLACES I WANT TO GO...THINGS I WANT TO SEE...
Z
SCHULZ

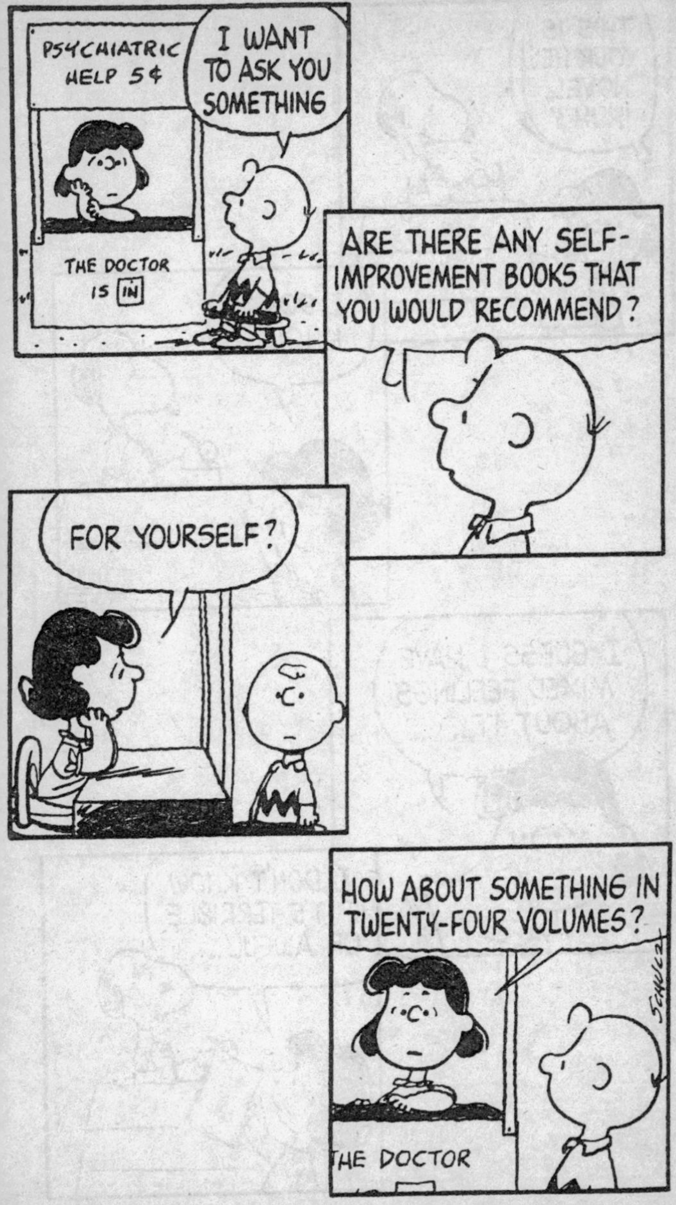
PSYCHIATRIC HELP 5¢
THE DOCTOR IS IN
I WANT TO ASK YOU SOMETHING
ARE THERE ANY SELF-IMPROVEMENT BOOKS THAT YOU WOULD RECOMMEND?
FOR YOURSELF?
HOW ABOUT SOMETHING IN TWENTY-FOUR VOLUMES?
THE DOCTOR
SCHULZ

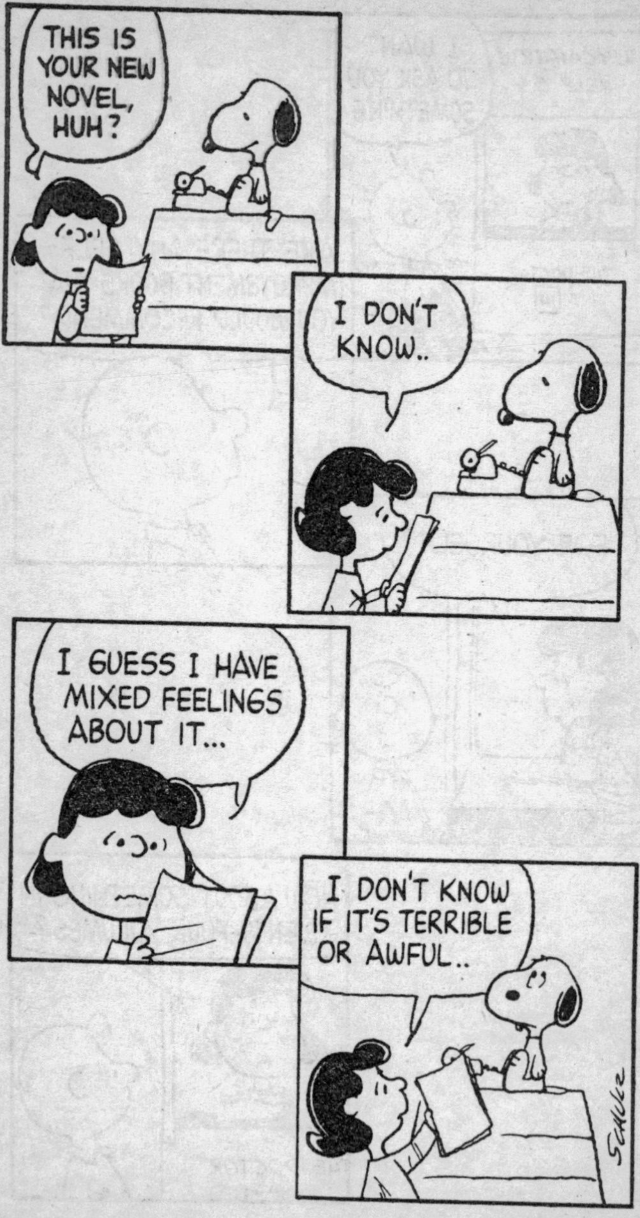
THIS IS YOUR NEW NOVEL, HUH?
I DON'T KNOW..
I GUESS I HAVE MIXED FEELINGS ABOUT IT...
I DON'T KNOW IF IT'S TERRIBLE OR AWFUL..
SCHULZ

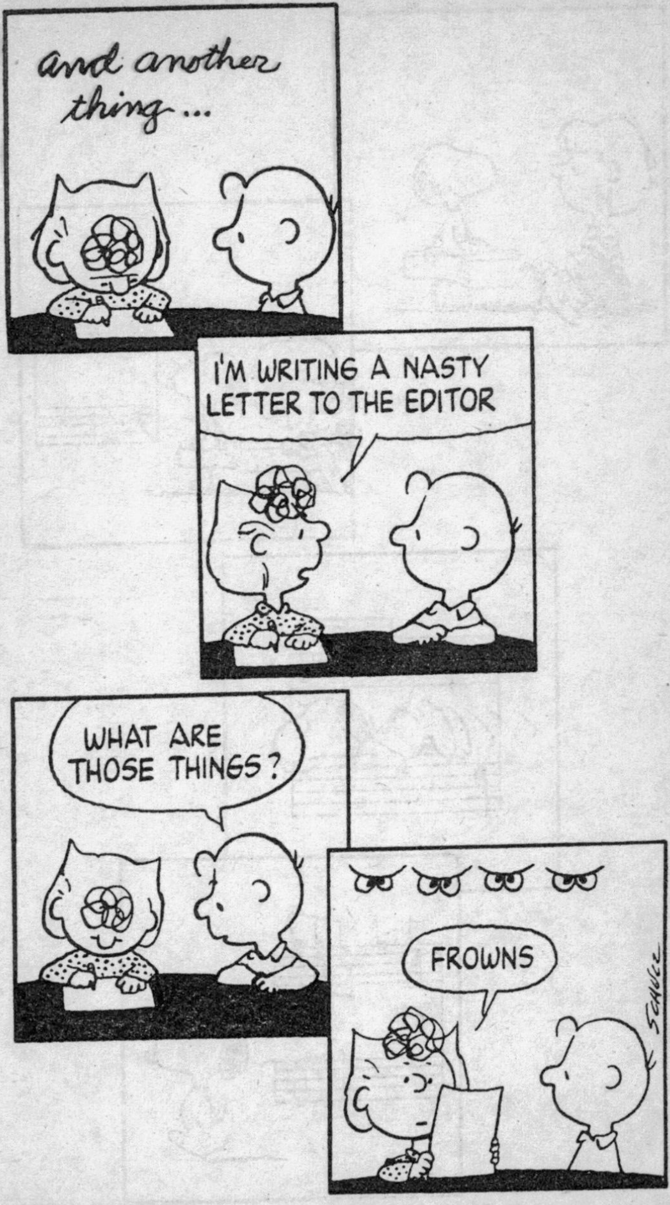
and another thing...
I'M WRITING A NASTY LETTER TO THE EDITOR
WHAT ARE THOSE THINGS?
FROWNS
SCHULZ

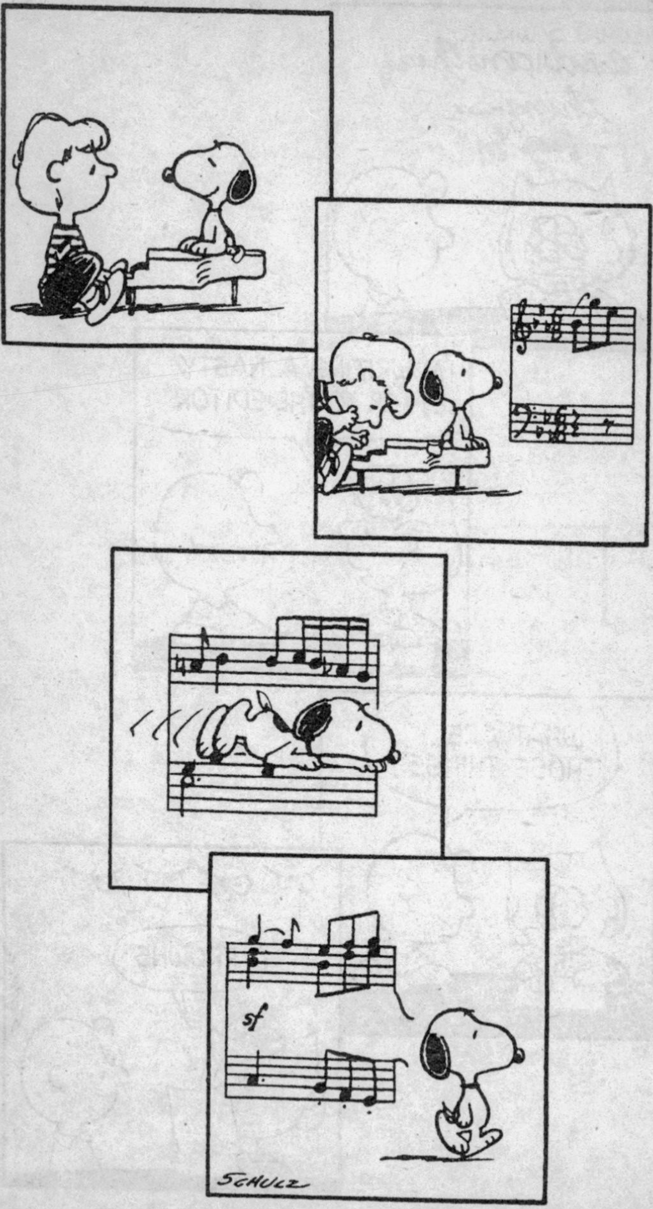
sf
SCHULZ

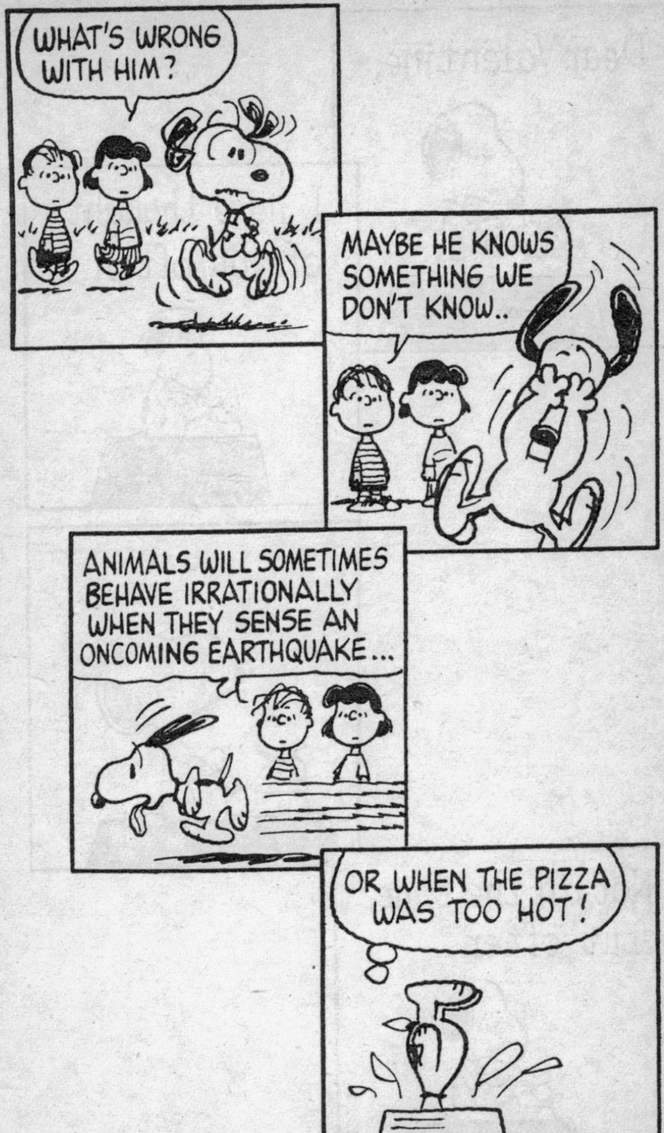
WHAT'S WRONG WITH HIM?
MAYBE HE KNOWS SOMETHING WE DON'T KNOW..
ANIMALS WILL SOMETIMES BEHAVE IRRATIONALLY WHEN THEY SENSE AN ONCOMING EARTHQUAKE...
OR WHEN THE PIZZA WAS TOO HOT!
SCHULZ

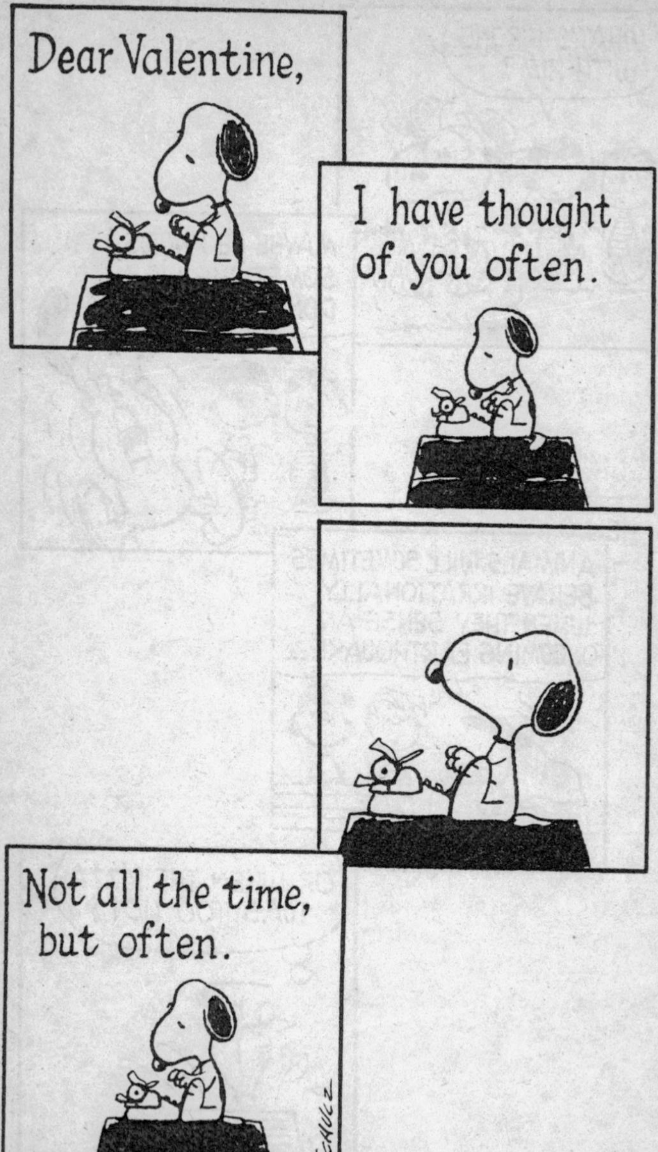
Dear Valentine,
I have thought of you often.
Not all the time, but often.
SCHULZ

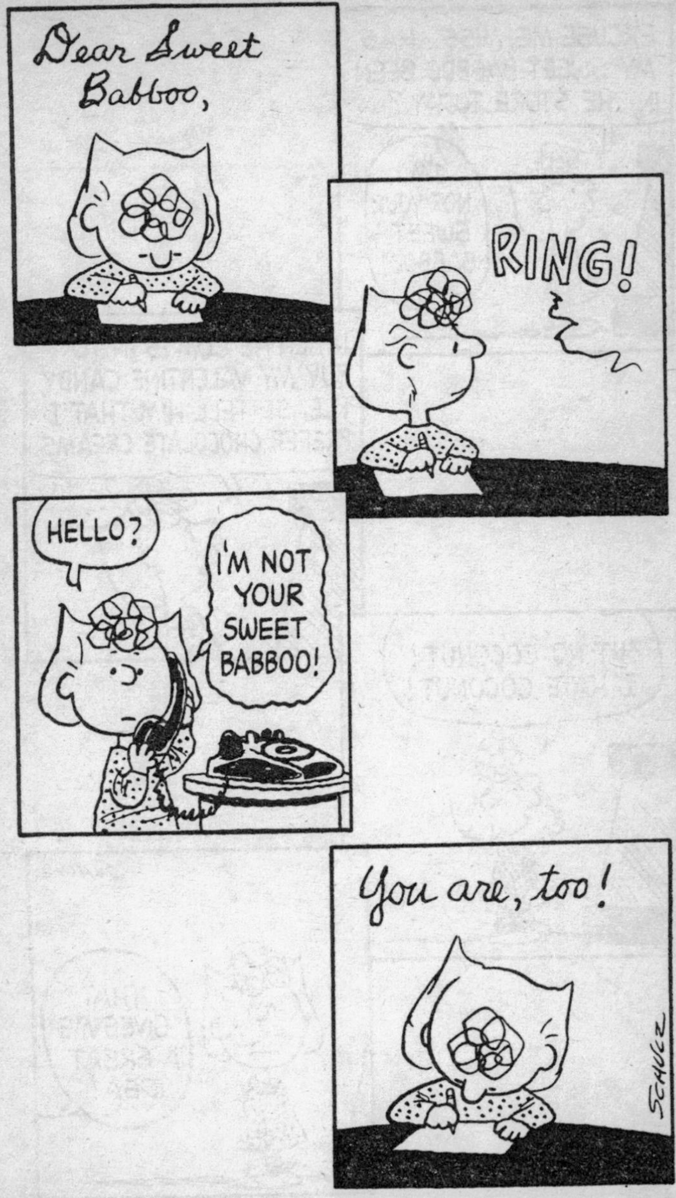
Dear Sweet Babboo,
RING!
HELLO?
I'M NOT YOUR SWEET BABBOO!
You are, too!
SCHULZ

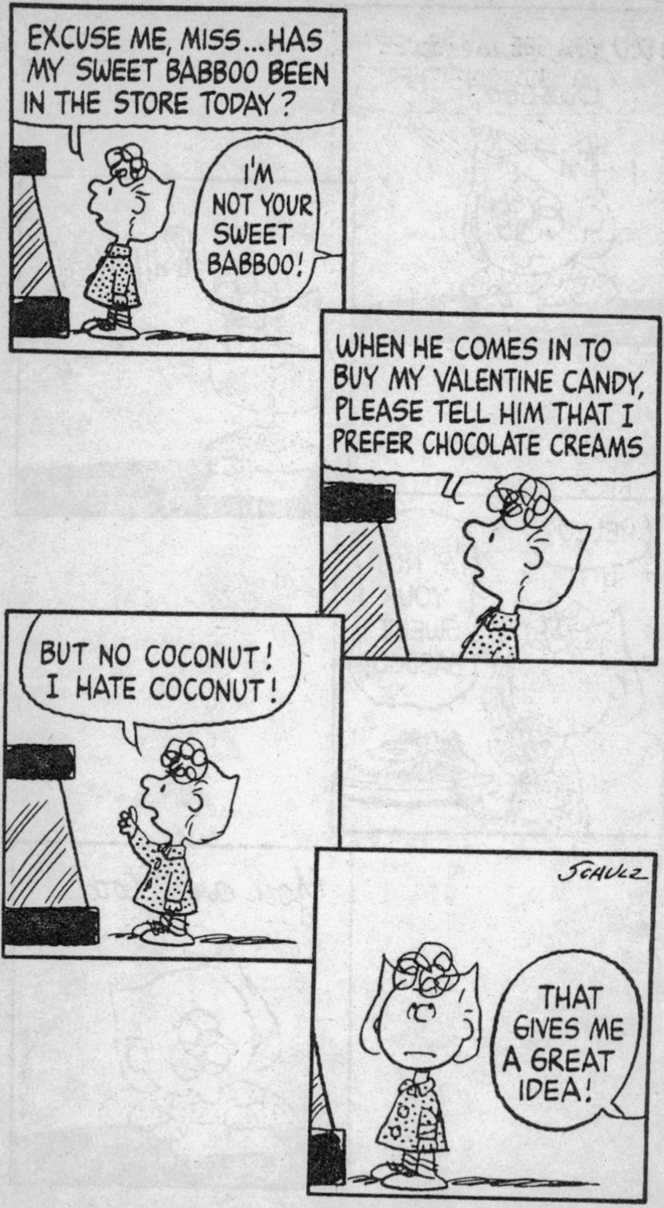
EXCUSE ME, MISS...HAS MY SWEET BABBOO BEEN IN THE STORE TODAY?
I'M NOT YOUR SWEET BABBOO!
WHEN HE COMES IN TO BUY MY VALENTINE CANDY, PLEASE TELL HIM THAT I PREFER CHOCOLATE CREAMS
BUT NO COCONUT! I HATE COCONUT!
SCHULZ
THAT GIVES ME A GREAT IDEA!

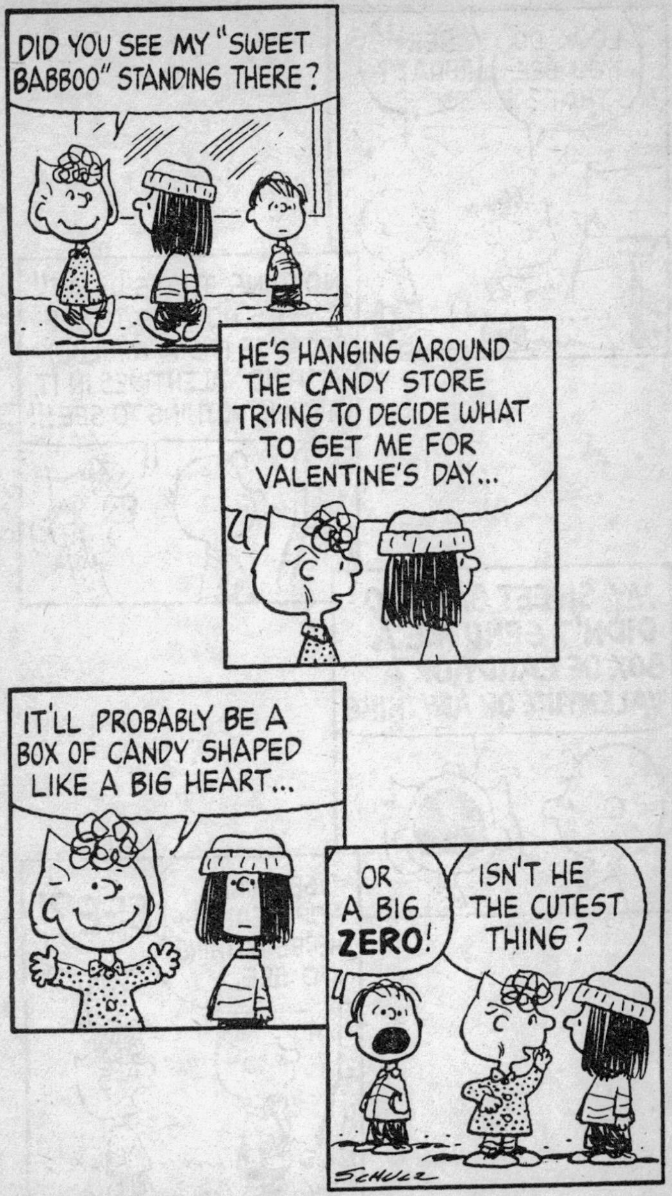
DID YOU SEE MY "SWEET BABBOO" STANDING THERE?
HE'S HANGING AROUND THE CANDY STORE TRYING TO DECIDE WHAT TO GET ME FOR VALENTINE'S DAY...
IT'LL PROBABLY BE A BOX OF CANDY SHAPED LIKE A BIG HEART...
ISN'T HE THE CUTEST THING?
OR A BIG **ZERO**!
SCHULZ

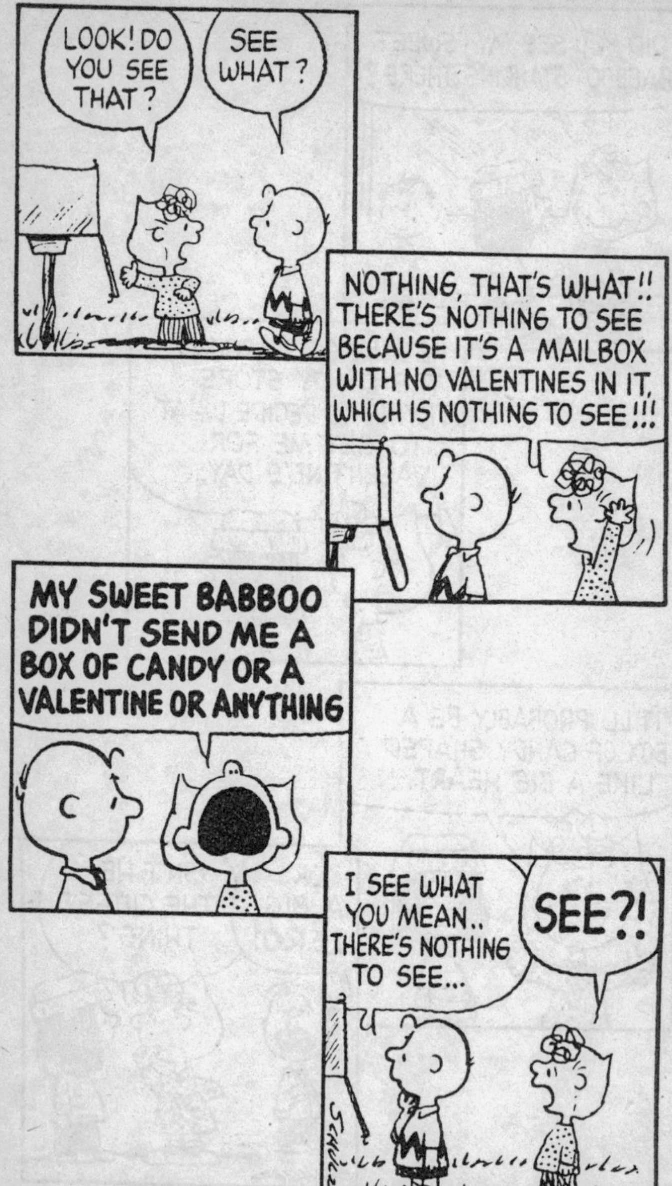
LOOK! DO YOU SEE THAT?
SEE WHAT?
NOTHING, THAT'S WHAT!! THERE'S NOTHING TO SEE BECAUSE IT'S A MAILBOX WITH NO VALENTINES IN IT, WHICH IS NOTHING TO SEE!!!
MY SWEET BABBOO DIDN'T SEND ME A BOX OF CANDY OR A VALENTINE OR ANYTHING
I SEE WHAT YOU MEAN.. THERE'S NOTHING TO SEE...
SEE?!
SCHULZ

SALLY, GET UP! YOU'RE GONNA BE LATE FOR SCHOOL!
LINUS DIDN'T SEND ME A VALENTINE, AND HE BROKE MY HEART AND I'M NEVER GOING TO SCHOOL AGAIN!
AND IF YOU SEE MY SWEET AN' SOUR BABBOO, PUNCH HIM IN THE NOSE!
"SWEET AN' SOUR"?
SCHULZ

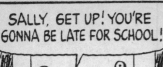

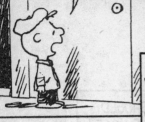

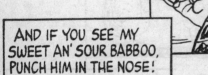

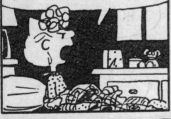

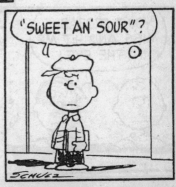

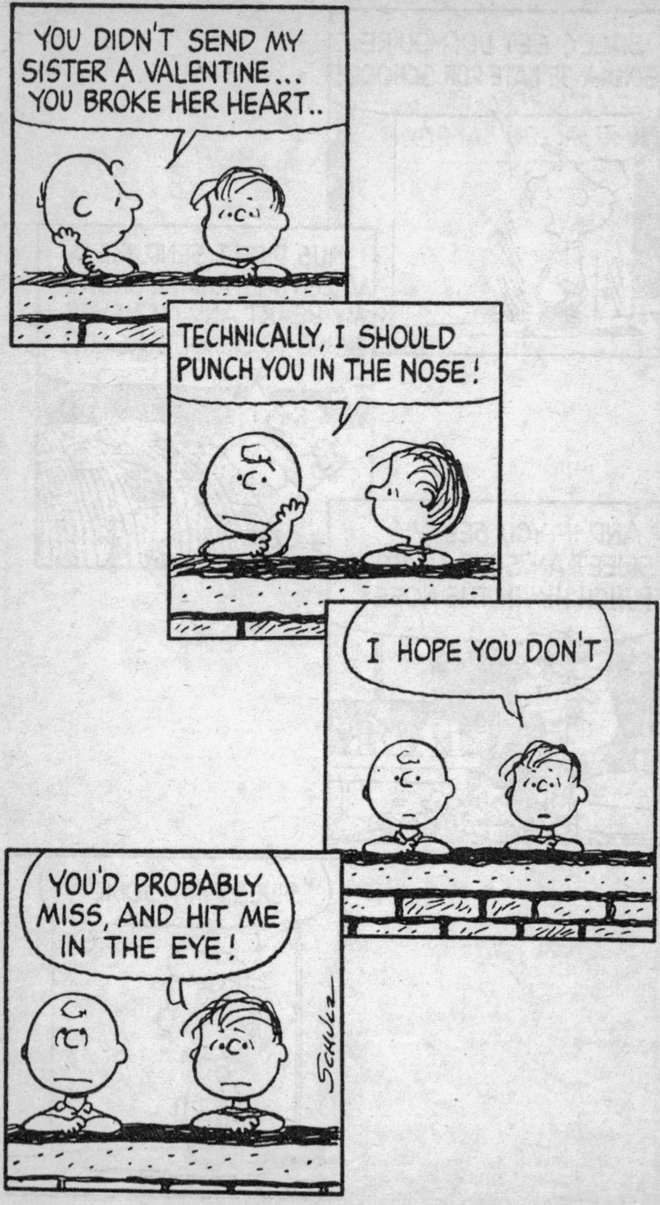
YOU DIDN'T SEND MY SISTER A VALENTINE... YOU BROKE HER HEART..
TECHNICALLY, I SHOULD PUNCH YOU IN THE NOSE!
I HOPE YOU DON'T
YOU'D PROBABLY MISS, AND HIT ME IN THE EYE!
SCHULZ

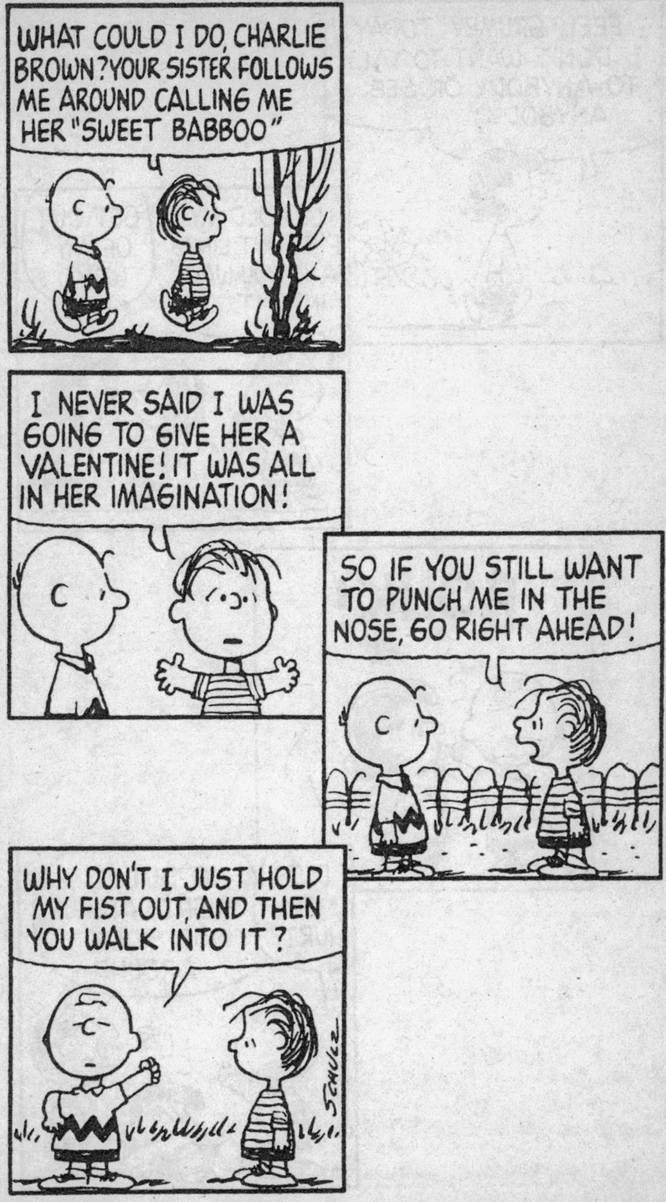

WHAT COULD I DO, CHARLIE BROWN? YOUR SISTER FOLLOWS ME AROUND CALLING ME HER "SWEET BABBOO"
I NEVER SAID I WAS GOING TO GIVE HER A VALENTINE! IT WAS ALL IN HER IMAGINATION!
SO IF YOU STILL WANT TO PUNCH ME IN THE NOSE, GO RIGHT AHEAD!
WHY DON'T I JUST HOLD MY FIST OUT, AND THEN YOU WALK INTO IT?
SCHULZ

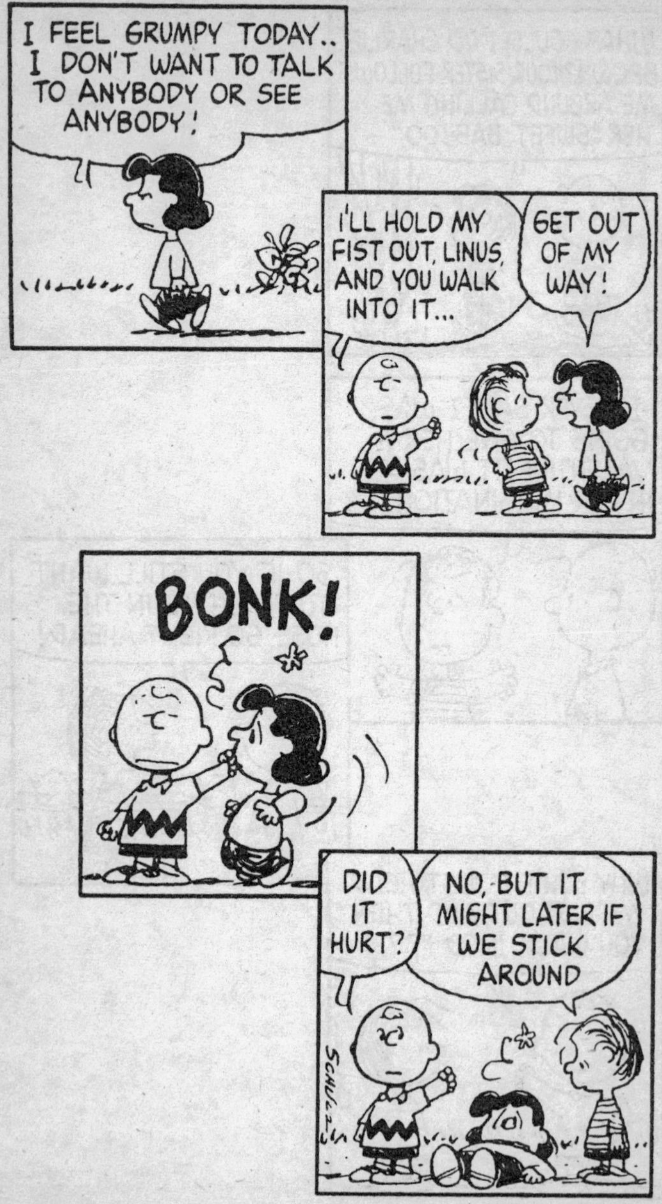
I FEEL GRUMPY TODAY.. I DON'T WANT TO TALK TO ANYBODY OR SEE ANYBODY!
I'LL HOLD MY FIST OUT, LINUS, AND YOU WALK INTO IT...
GET OUT OF MY WAY!
BONK!
DID IT HURT?
NO, BUT IT MIGHT LATER IF WE STICK AROUND
SCHULZ

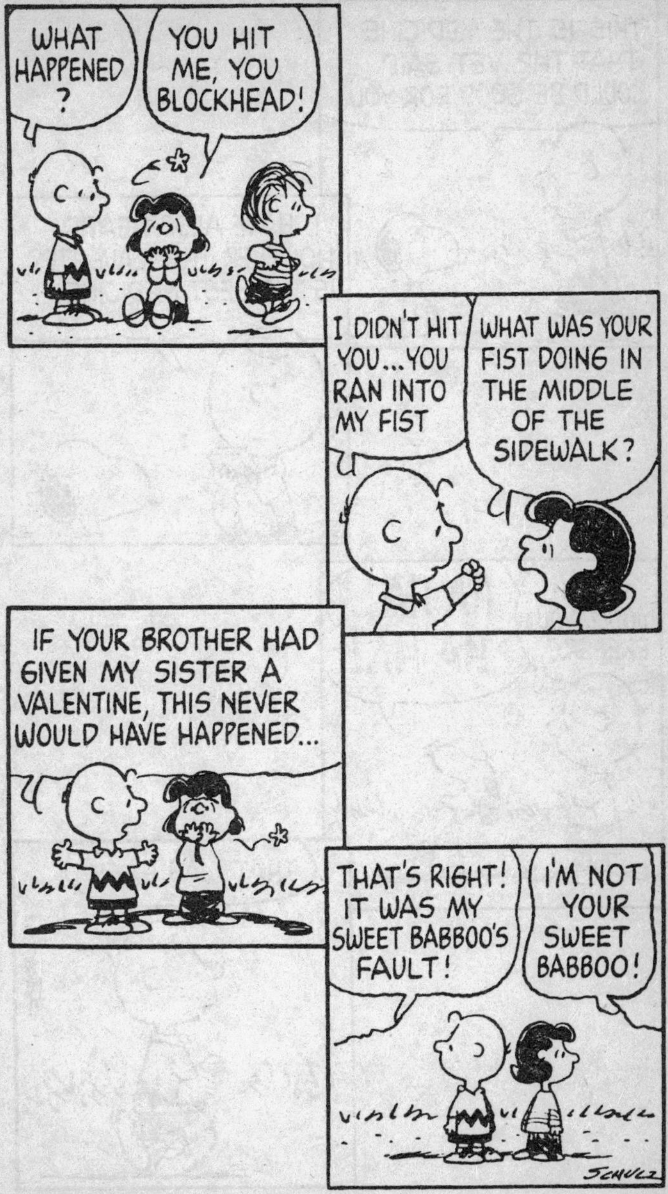
WHAT HAPPENED ?
YOU HIT ME, YOU BLOCKHEAD!
I DIDN'T HIT YOU...YOU RAN INTO MY FIST
WHAT WAS YOUR FIST DOING IN THE MIDDLE OF THE SIDEWALK?
IF YOUR BROTHER HAD GIVEN MY SISTER A VALENTINE, THIS NEVER WOULD HAVE HAPPENED...
THAT'S RIGHT! IT WAS MY SWEET BABBOO'S FAULT!
I'M NOT YOUR SWEET BABBOO!
SCHULZ

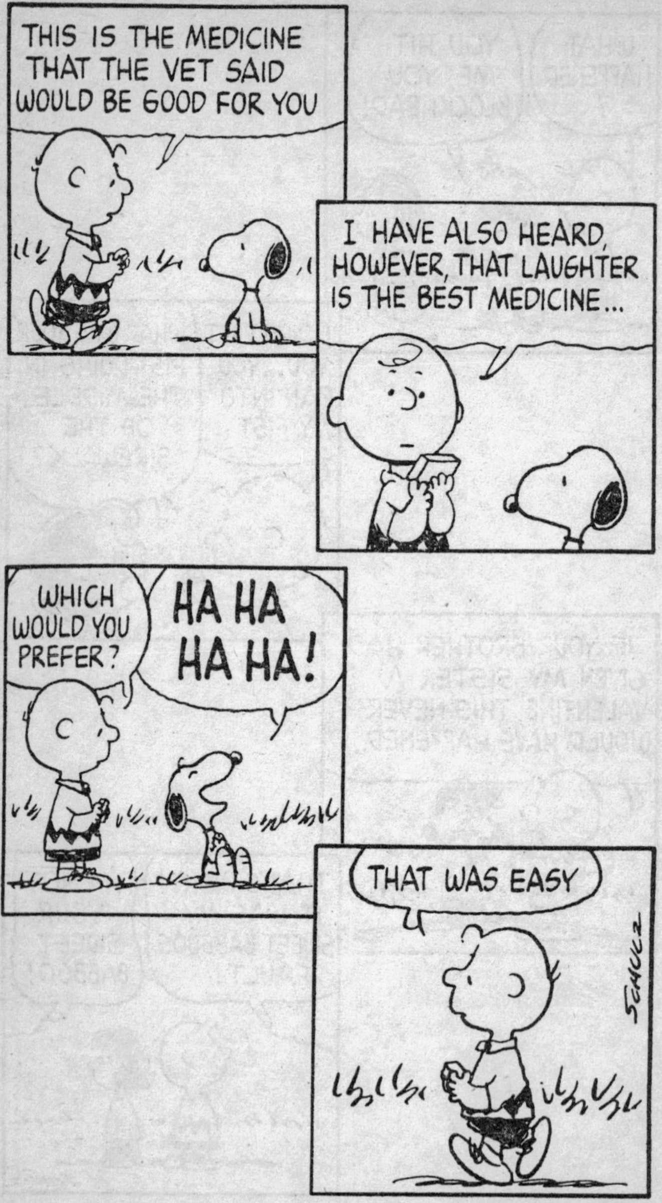
THIS IS THE MEDICINE THAT THE VET SAID WOULD BE GOOD FOR YOU
I HAVE ALSO HEARD, HOWEVER, THAT LAUGHTER IS THE BEST MEDICINE...
WHICH WOULD YOU PREFER?
HA HA HA HA!
THAT WAS EASY
SCHULZ

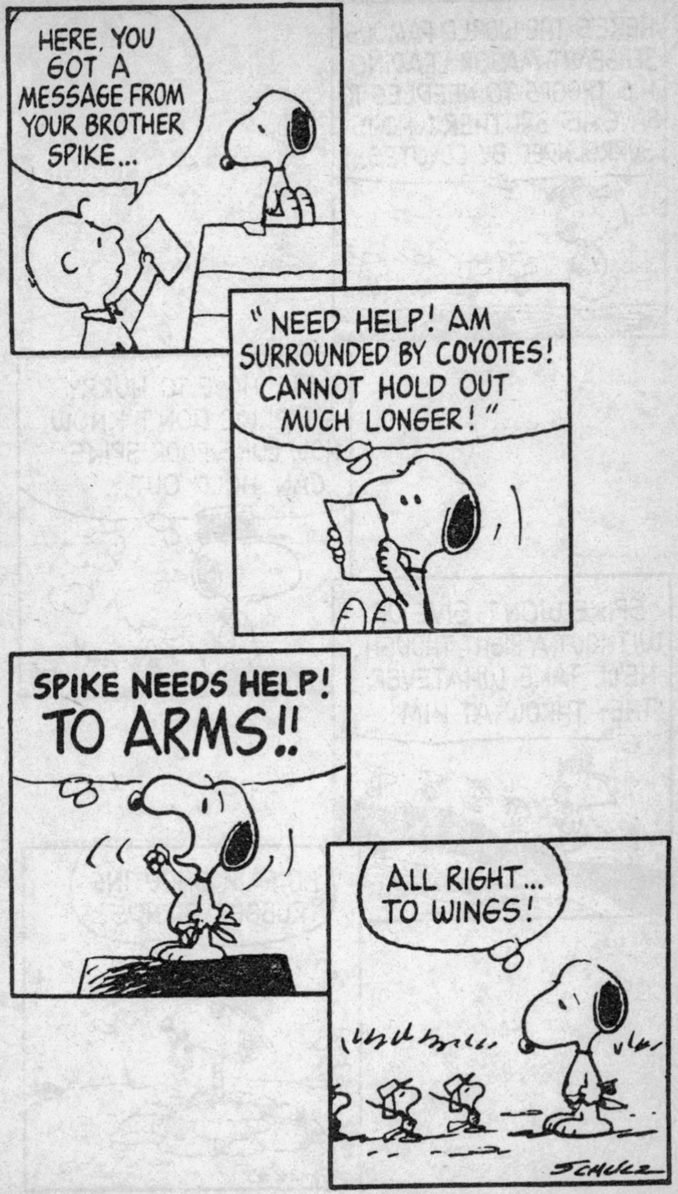
HERE, YOU GOT A MESSAGE FROM YOUR BROTHER SPIKE...
"NEED HELP! AM SURROUNDED BY COYOTES! CANNOT HOLD OUT MUCH LONGER!"
SPIKE NEEDS HELP! TO ARMS!!
ALL RIGHT... TO WINGS!
SCHULZ

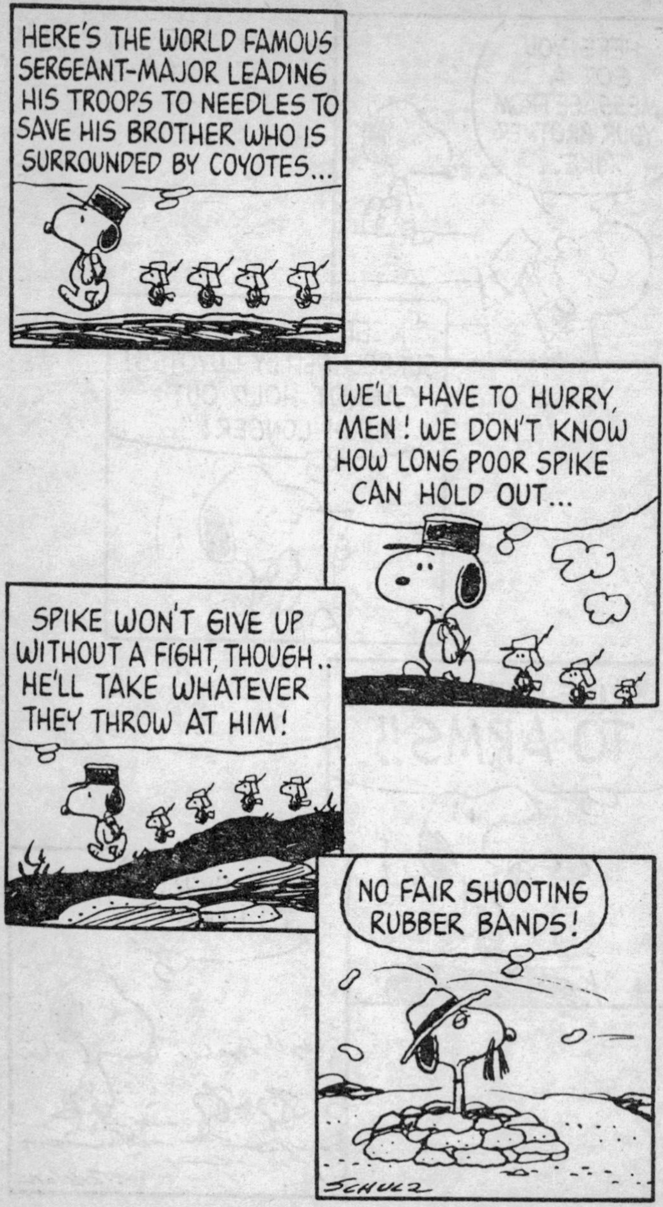
HERE'S THE WORLD FAMOUS SERGEANT-MAJOR LEADING HIS TROOPS TO NEEDLES TO SAVE HIS BROTHER WHO IS SURROUNDED BY COYOTES...
WE'LL HAVE TO HURRY, MEN! WE DON'T KNOW HOW LONG POOR SPIKE CAN HOLD OUT...
SPIKE WON'T GIVE UP WITHOUT A FIGHT, THOUGH.. HE'LL TAKE WHATEVER THEY THROW AT HIM!
NO FAIR SHOOTING RUBBER BANDS!
SCHULZ

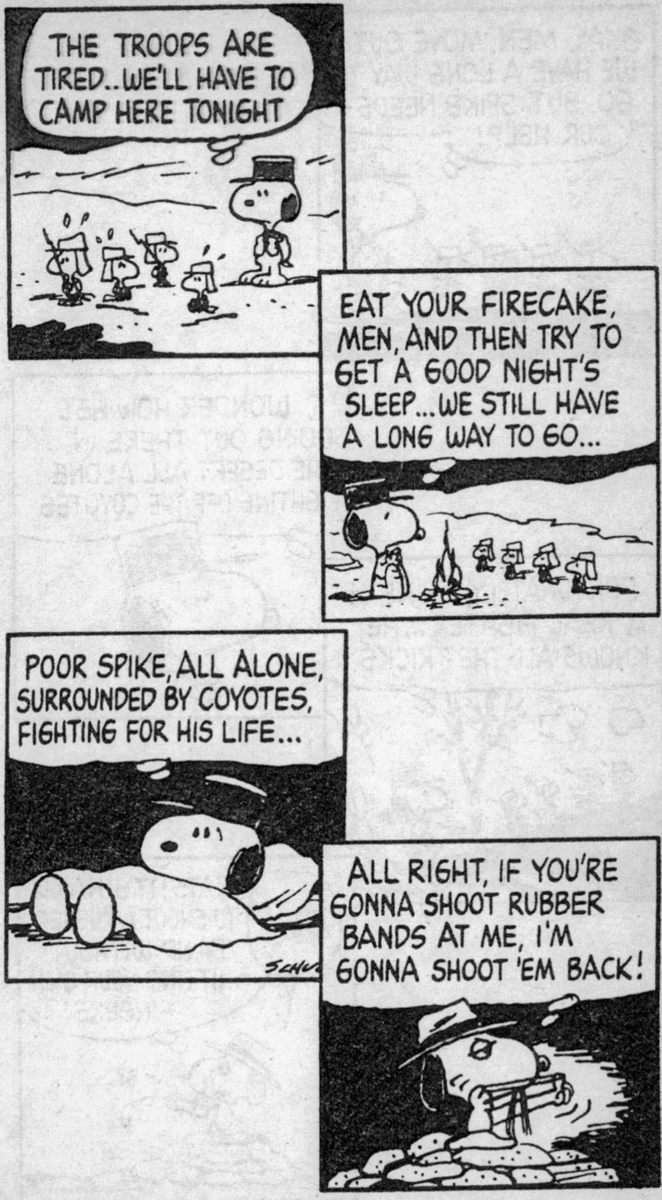
THE TROOPS ARE TIRED..WE'LL HAVE TO CAMP HERE TONIGHT
EAT YOUR FIRECAKE, MEN, AND THEN TRY TO GET A GOOD NIGHT'S SLEEP...WE STILL HAVE A LONG WAY TO GO...
POOR SPIKE, ALL ALONE, SURROUNDED BY COYOTES, FIGHTING FOR HIS LIFE...
ALL RIGHT, IF YOU'RE GONNA SHOOT RUBBER BANDS AT ME, I'M GONNA SHOOT 'EM BACK!

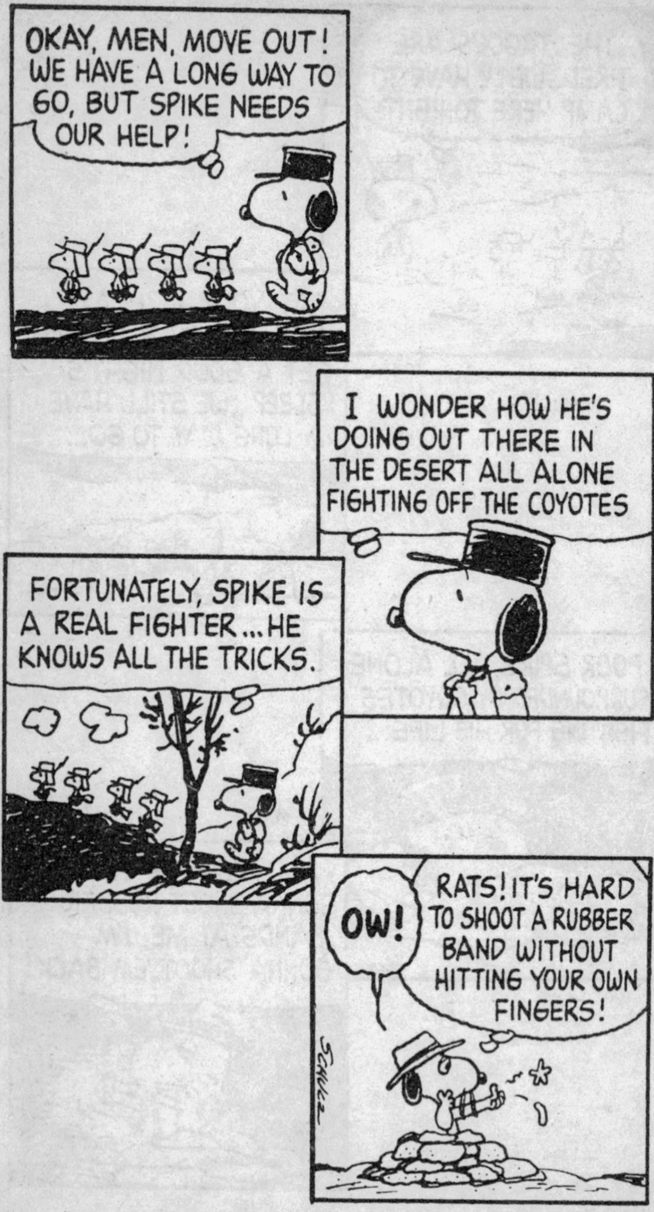
OKAY, MEN, MOVE OUT! WE HAVE A LONG WAY TO GO, BUT SPIKE NEEDS OUR HELP!
I WONDER HOW HE'S DOING OUT THERE IN THE DESERT ALL ALONE FIGHTING OFF THE COYOTES
FORTUNATELY, SPIKE IS A REAL FIGHTER... HE KNOWS ALL THE TRICKS.
OW!
RATS! IT'S HARD TO SHOOT A RUBBER BAND WITHOUT HITTING YOUR OWN FINGERS!
SCHULZ

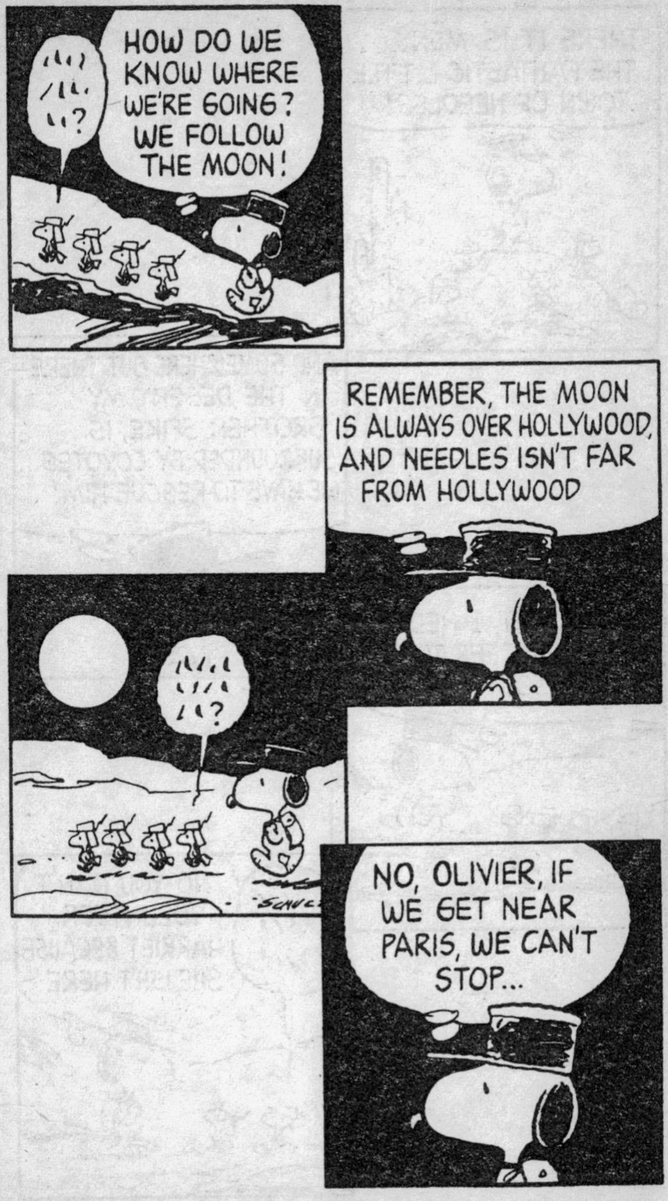
HOW DO WE KNOW WHERE WE'RE GOING? WE FOLLOW THE MOON!
REMEMBER, THE MOON IS ALWAYS OVER HOLLYWOOD, AND NEEDLES ISN'T FAR FROM HOLLYWOOD
NO, OLIVIER, IF WE GET NEAR PARIS, WE CAN'T STOP...

THERE IT IS, MEN.. THE FANTASTIC LITTLE TOWN OF NEEDLES!
AND SOMEWHERE OUT THERE IN THE DESERT, MY BROTHER, SPIKE, IS SURROUNDED BY COYOTES... WE HAVE TO RESCUE HIM!
ALL RIGHT, I NEED ONE VOLUNTEER TO ACT AS SCOUT...
NO, YOU CAN'T VOLUNTEER HARRIET BECAUSE SHE ISN'T HERE
SCHULZ

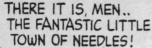

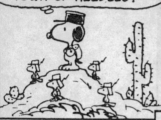

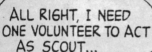

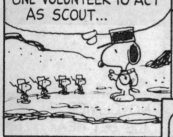

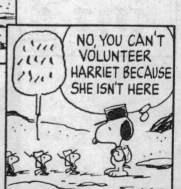

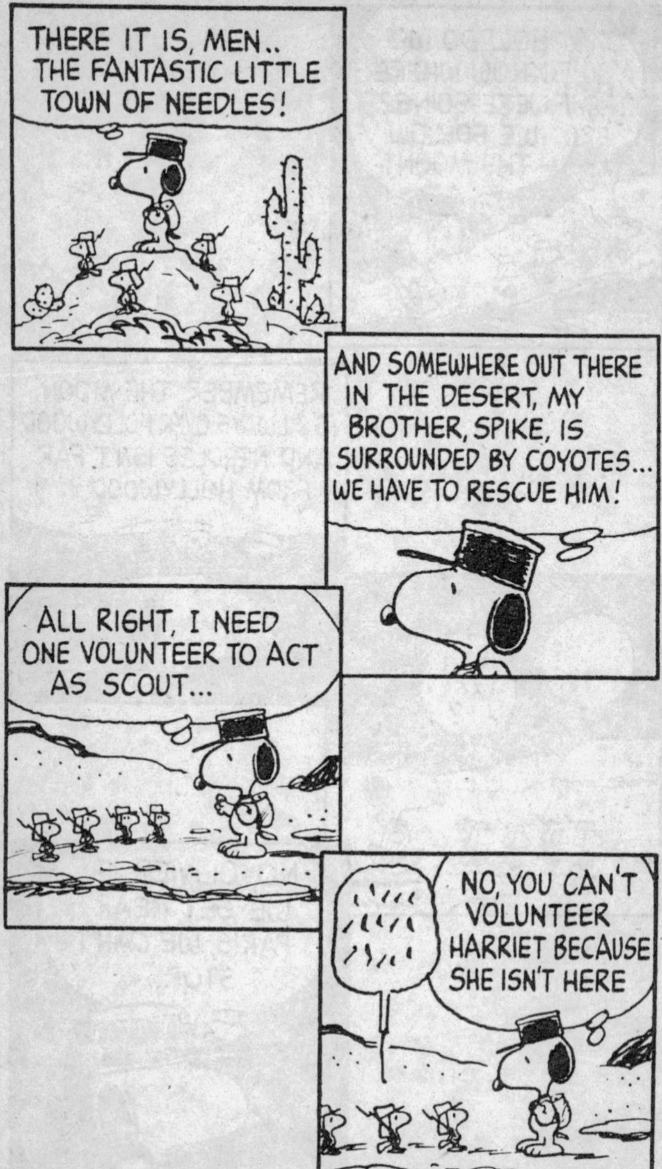

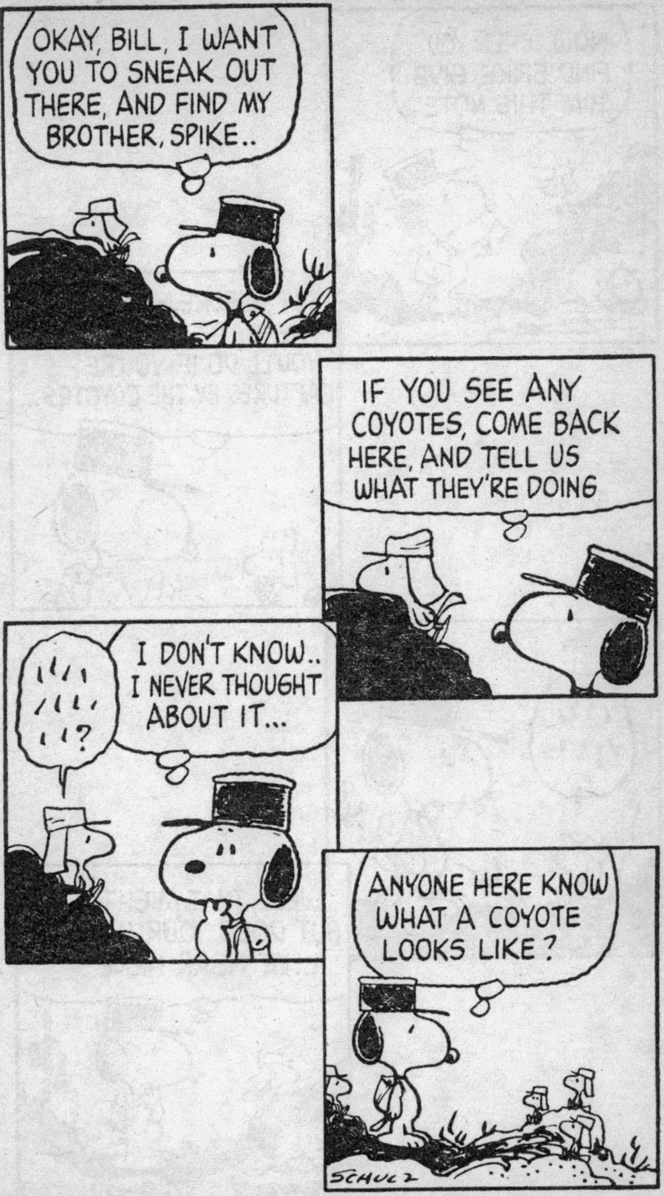
OKAY, BILL, I WANT YOU TO SNEAK OUT THERE, AND FIND MY BROTHER, SPIKE..
IF YOU SEE ANY COYOTES, COME BACK HERE, AND TELL US WHAT THEY'RE DOING
?
I DON'T KNOW.. I NEVER THOUGHT ABOUT IT...
ANYONE HERE KNOW WHAT A COYOTE LOOKS LIKE?
SCHULZ

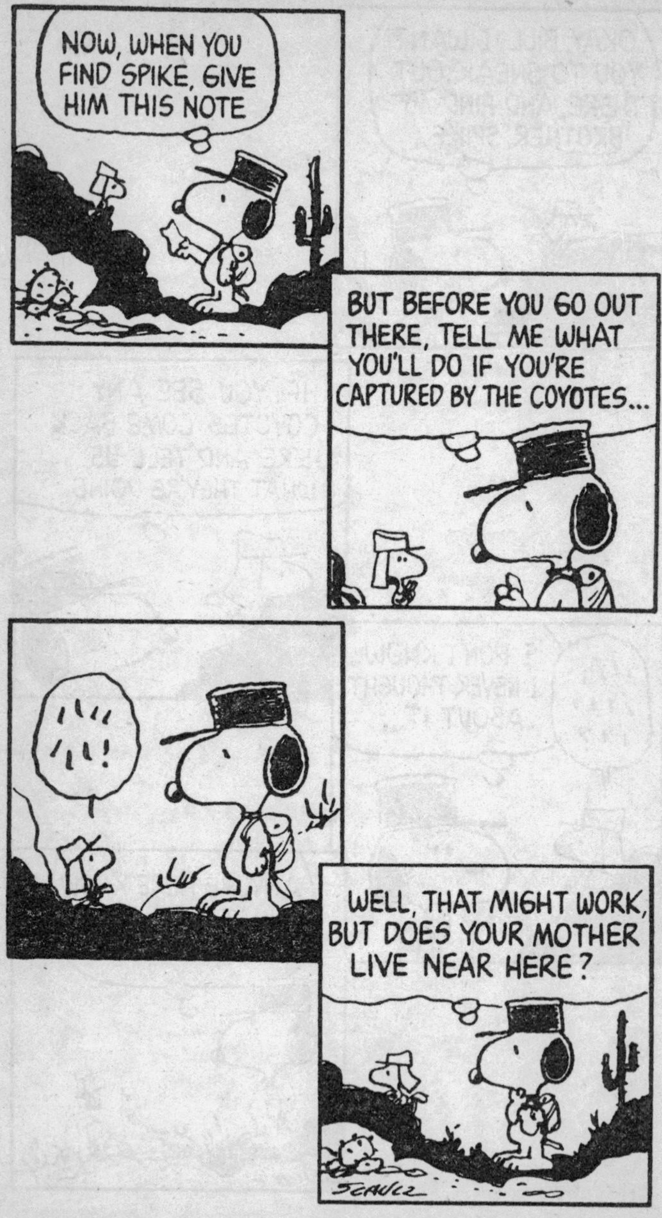
NOW, WHEN YOU FIND SPIKE, GIVE HIM THIS NOTE
BUT BEFORE YOU GO OUT THERE, TELL ME WHAT YOU'LL DO IF YOU'RE CAPTURED BY THE COYOTES...
WELL, THAT MIGHT WORK, BUT DOES YOUR MOTHER LIVE NEAR HERE?
SCHULZ

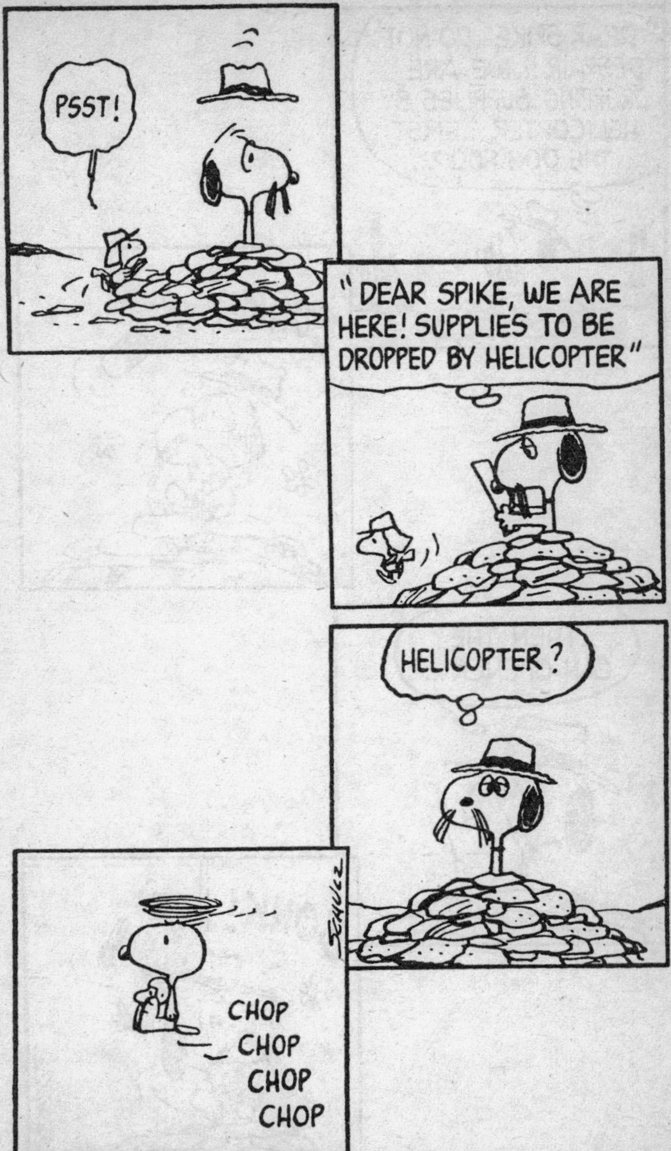
PSST!
"DEAR SPIKE, WE ARE HERE! SUPPLIES TO BE DROPPED BY HELICOPTER"
HELICOPTER?
SCHULZ
CHOP
CHOP
CHOP
CHOP

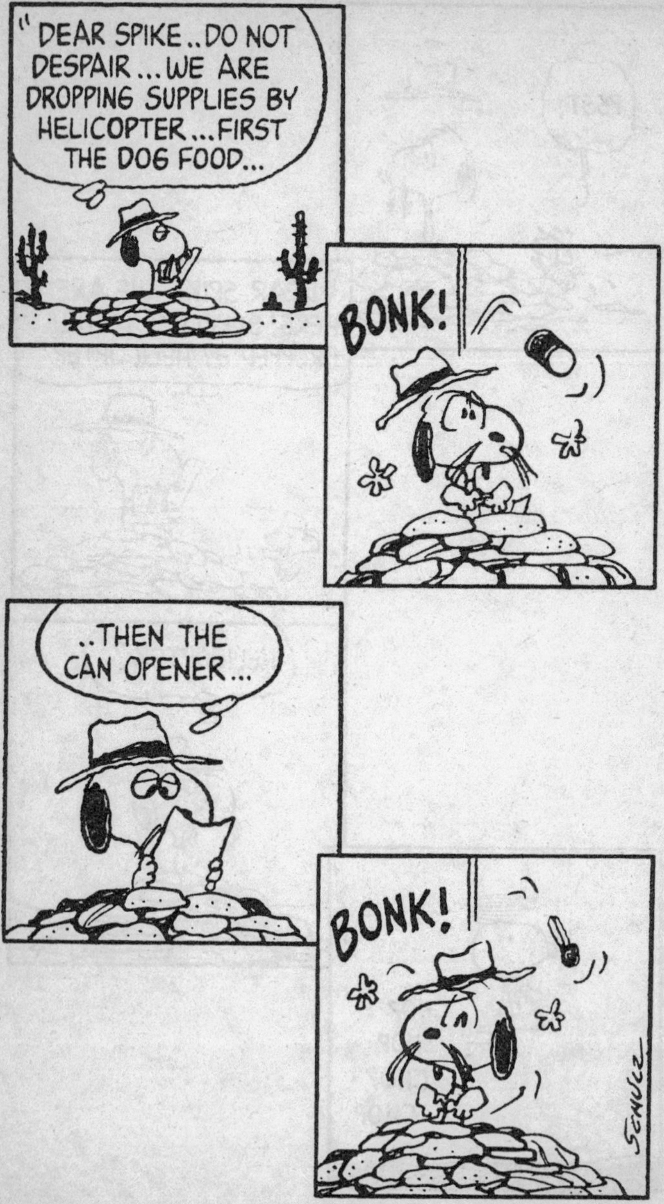
"DEAR SPIKE..DO NOT DESPAIR...WE ARE DROPPING SUPPLIES BY HELICOPTER...FIRST THE DOG FOOD...
BONK!
..THEN THE CAN OPENER...
BONK!
SCHULZ

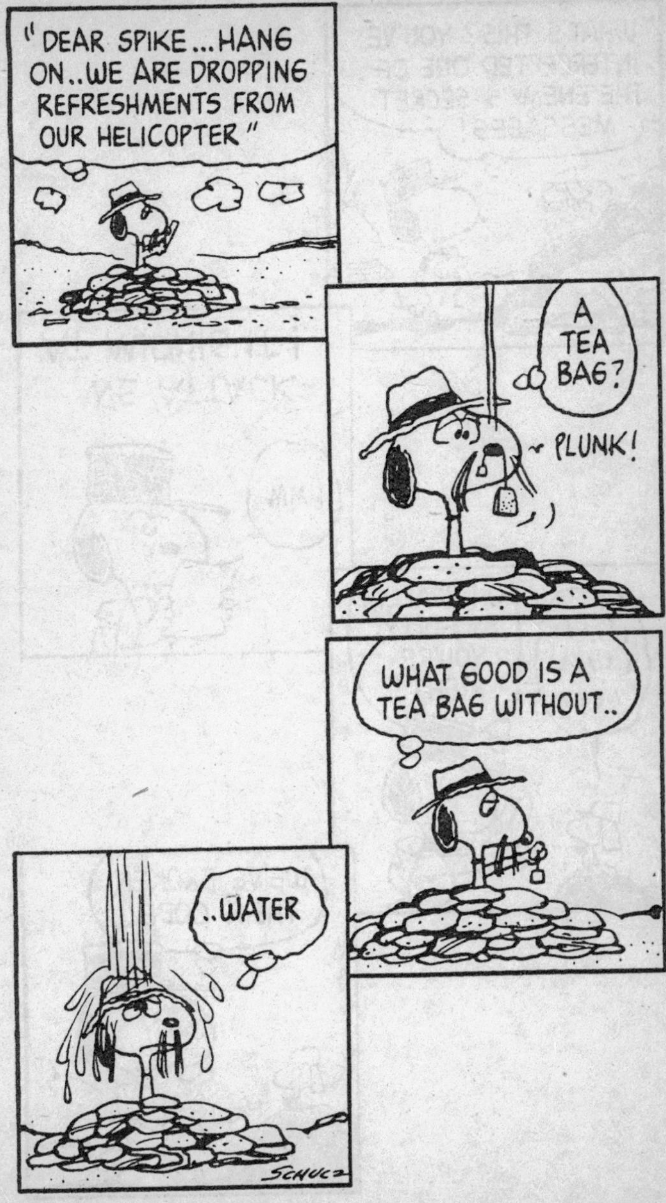
"DEAR SPIKE...HANG ON..WE ARE DROPPING REFRESHMENTS FROM OUR HELICOPTER"
A TEA BAG?
PLUNK!
WHAT GOOD IS A TEA BAG WITHOUT..
..WATER
SCHULZ

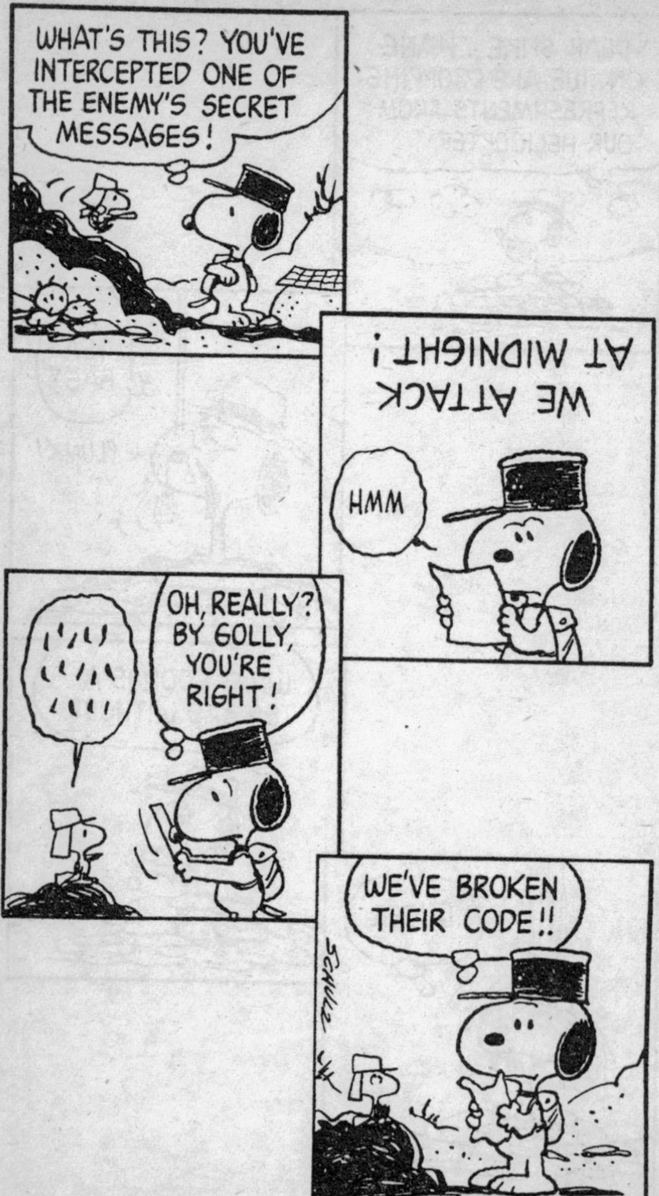
WHAT'S THIS? YOU'VE INTERCEPTED ONE OF THE ENEMY'S SECRET MESSAGES!
WE ATTACK AT MIDNIGHT!
HMM
OH, REALLY? BY GOLLY, YOU'RE RIGHT!
WE'VE BROKEN THEIR CODE!!
SCHULZ

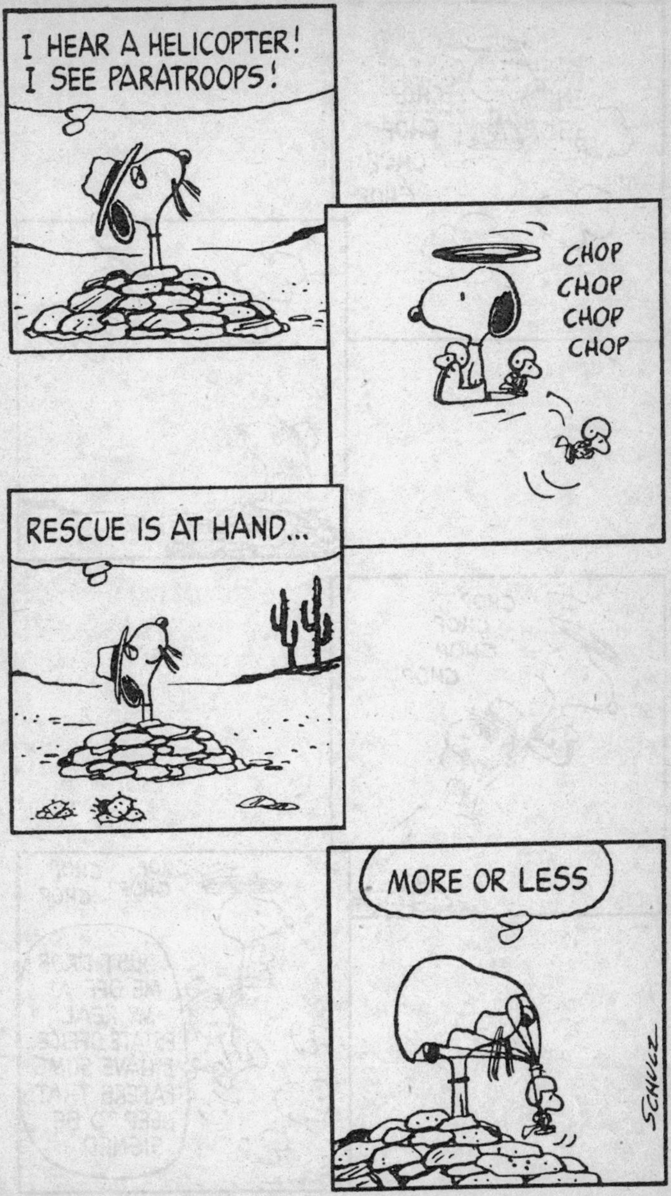
I HEAR A HELICOPTER! I SEE PARATROOPS!
CHOP CHOP CHOP CHOP
RESCUE IS AT HAND...
MORE OR LESS
SCHULZ

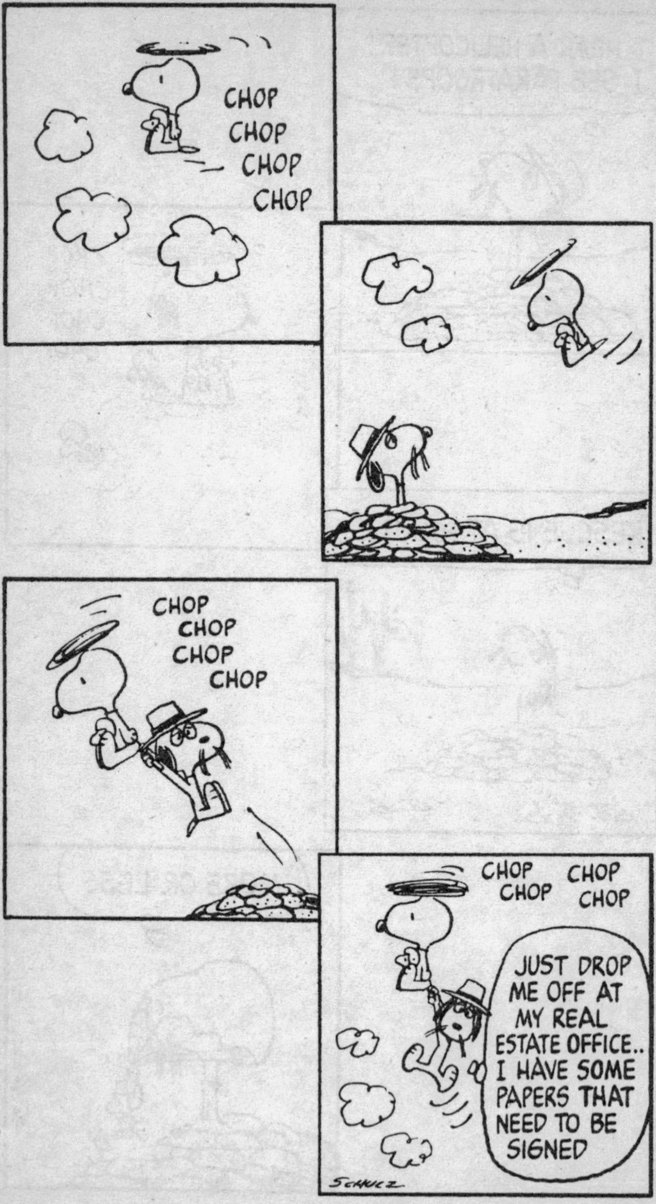
CHOP
CHOP
CHOP
CHOP
CHOP
CHOP
CHOP
CHOP
CHOP
CHOP
CHOP
CHOP
JUST DROP ME OFF AT MY REAL ESTATE OFFICE.. I HAVE SOME PAPERS THAT NEED TO BE SIGNED
SCHULZ

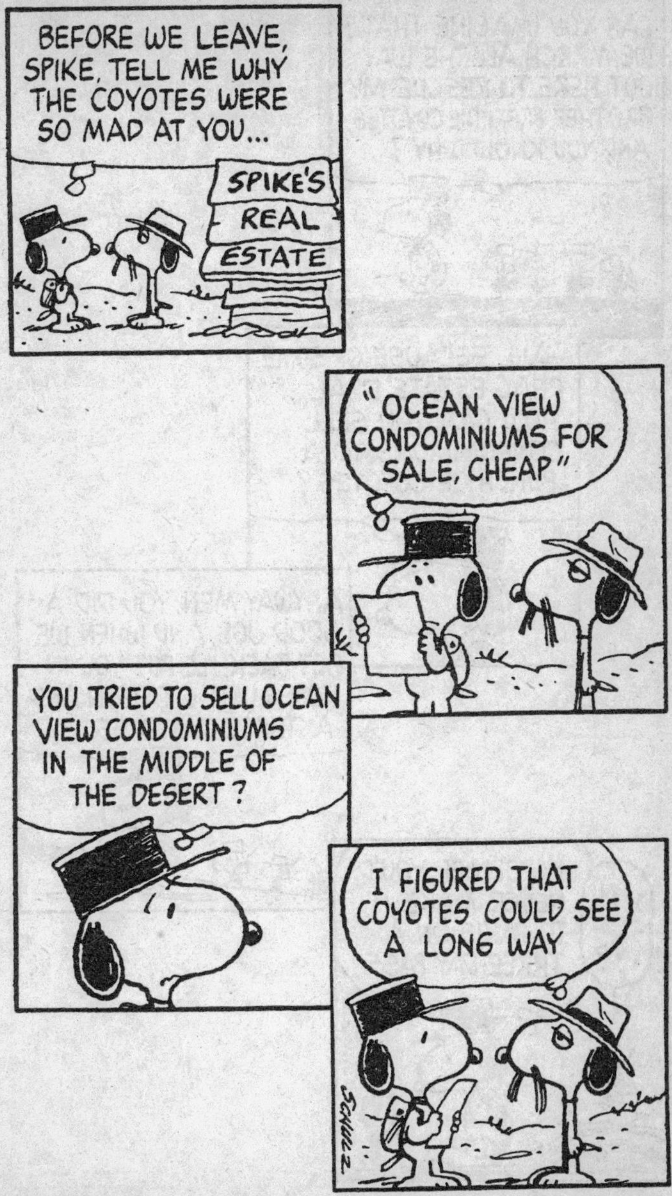

BEFORE WE LEAVE, SPIKE, TELL ME WHY THE COYOTES WERE SO MAD AT YOU...
SPIKE'S REAL ESTATE
"OCEAN VIEW CONDOMINIUMS FOR SALE, CHEAP"
YOU TRIED TO SELL OCEAN VIEW CONDOMINIUMS IN THE MIDDLE OF THE DESERT?
I FIGURED THAT COYOTES COULD SEE A LONG WAY
SCHULZ

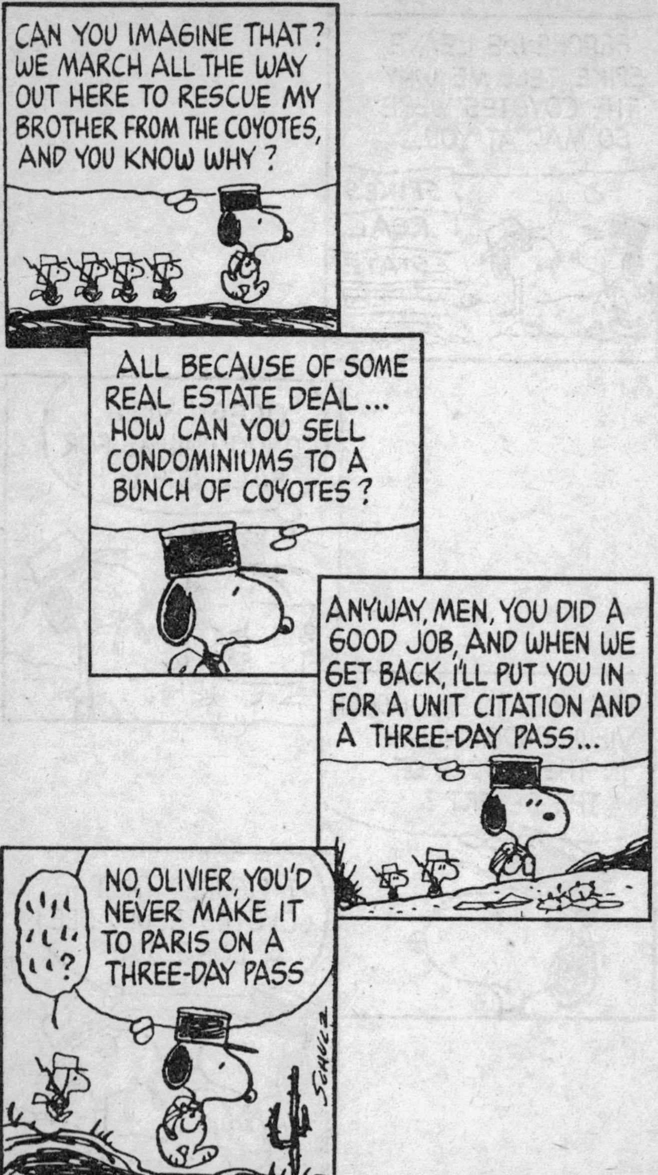
CAN YOU IMAGINE THAT? WE MARCH ALL THE WAY OUT HERE TO RESCUE MY BROTHER FROM THE COYOTES, AND YOU KNOW WHY?
ALL BECAUSE OF SOME REAL ESTATE DEAL... HOW CAN YOU SELL CONDOMINIUMS TO A BUNCH OF COYOTES?
ANYWAY, MEN, YOU DID A GOOD JOB, AND WHEN WE GET BACK, I'LL PUT YOU IN FOR A UNIT CITATION AND A THREE-DAY PASS...
?
NO, OLIVIER, YOU'D NEVER MAKE IT TO PARIS ON A THREE-DAY PASS
SCHULZ

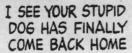

I SEE YOUR STUPID DOG HAS FINALLY COME BACK HOME

I DON'T SEE HOW HE FINDS HIS WAY AROUND LIKE HE DOES...

DOGS HAVE A FANTASTIC SENSE OF DIRECTION AND VERY GOOD MEMORIES

IS THIS WHERE I LIVE?

SCHULZ

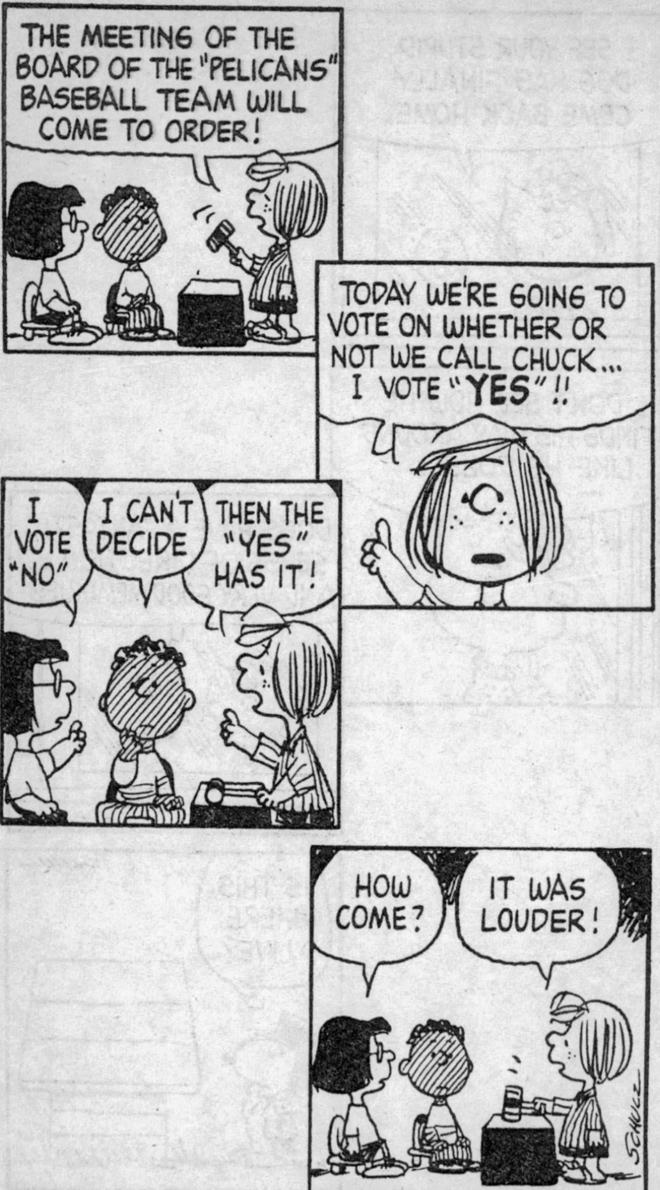
THE MEETING OF THE BOARD OF THE "PELICANS" BASEBALL TEAM WILL COME TO ORDER!
TODAY WE'RE GOING TO VOTE ON WHETHER OR NOT WE CALL CHUCK... I VOTE "YES"!!
I VOTE "NO"
I CAN'T DECIDE
THEN THE "YES" HAS IT!
HOW COME?
IT WAS LOUDER!
SCHULZ

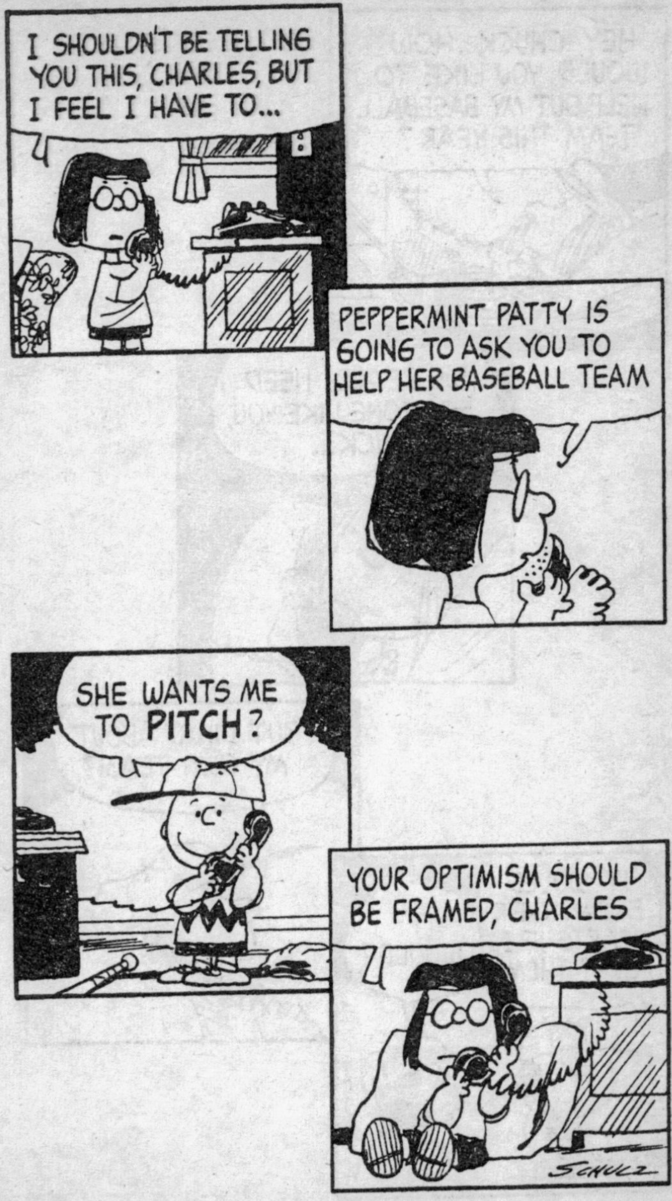
I SHOULDN'T BE TELLING YOU THIS, CHARLES, BUT I FEEL I HAVE TO...
PEPPERMINT PATTY IS GOING TO ASK YOU TO HELP HER BASEBALL TEAM
SHE WANTS ME TO **PITCH**?
YOUR OPTIMISM SHOULD BE FRAMED, CHARLES
SCHULZ

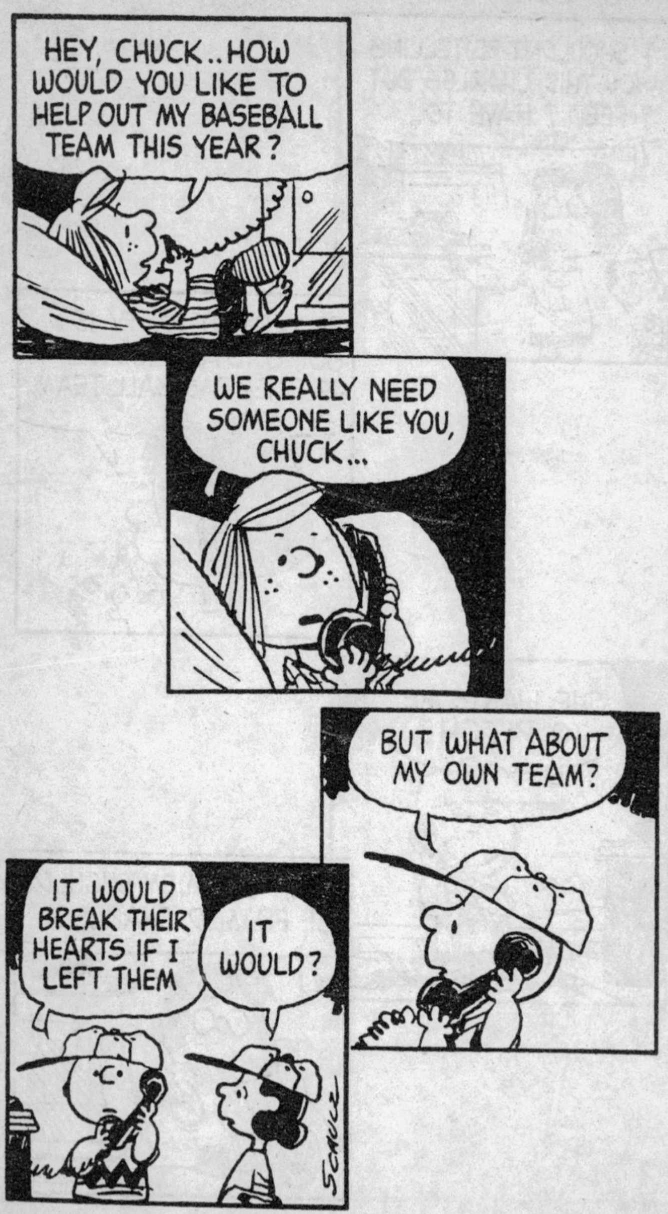
HEY, CHUCK..HOW WOULD YOU LIKE TO HELP OUT MY BASEBALL TEAM THIS YEAR?
WE REALLY NEED SOMEONE LIKE YOU, CHUCK...
BUT WHAT ABOUT MY OWN TEAM?
IT WOULD BREAK THEIR HEARTS IF I LEFT THEM
IT WOULD?
SCHULZ

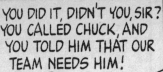

YOU DID IT, DIDN'T YOU, SIR? YOU CALLED CHUCK, AND YOU TOLD HIM THAT OUR TEAM NEEDS HIM!

WELL, WE DO, MARCIE

YES, BUT NOT FOR WHAT HE THINKS!

HE THINKS HE'S GOING TO BE THE PITCHER OR PLAY RIGHT WING, OR LINEBACKER OR GOALIE OR SOMETHING!

LOOK, MARCIE, YOU'VE GOT ME SO UPSET MY HAIR IS FALLING OUT

IT'S EITHER A THYROID PROBLEM OR GUILT, SIR

SCHULZ

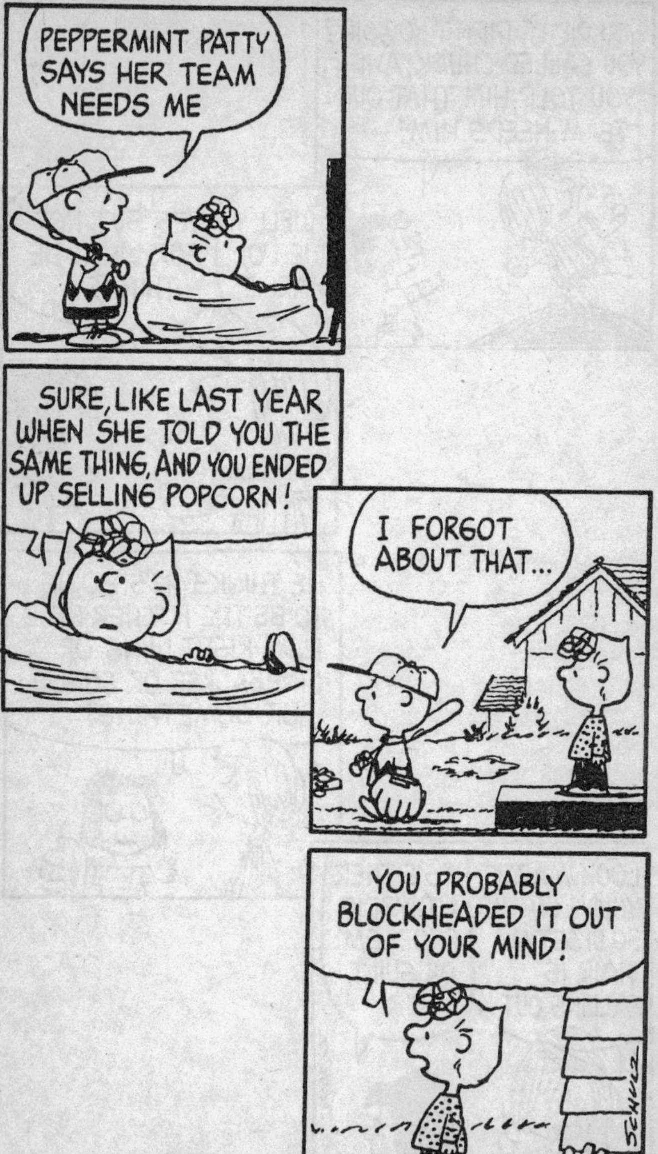
PEPPERMINT PATTY SAYS HER TEAM NEEDS ME
SURE, LIKE LAST YEAR WHEN SHE TOLD YOU THE SAME THING, AND YOU ENDED UP SELLING POPCORN!
I FORGOT ABOUT THAT...
YOU PROBABLY BLOCKHEADED IT OUT OF YOUR MIND!
SCHULZ

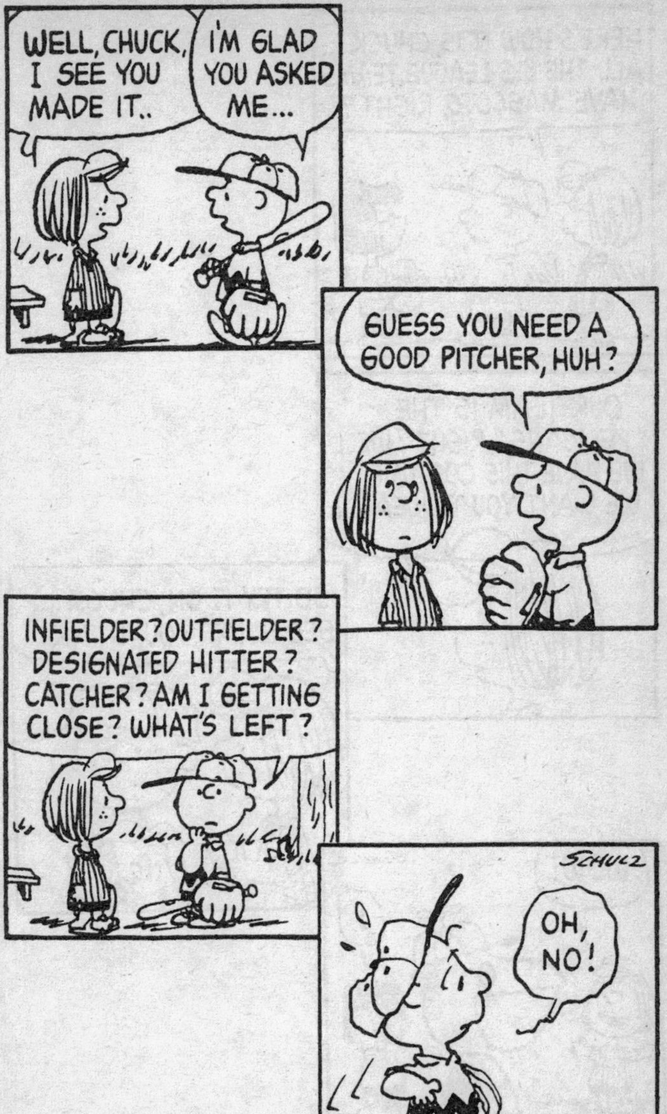
WELL, CHUCK, I SEE YOU MADE IT..
I'M GLAD YOU ASKED ME...
GUESS YOU NEED A GOOD PITCHER, HUH?
INFIELDER? OUTFIELDER? DESIGNATED HITTER? CATCHER? AM I GETTING CLOSE? WHAT'S LEFT?
SCHULZ
OH, NO!

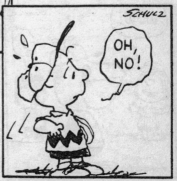

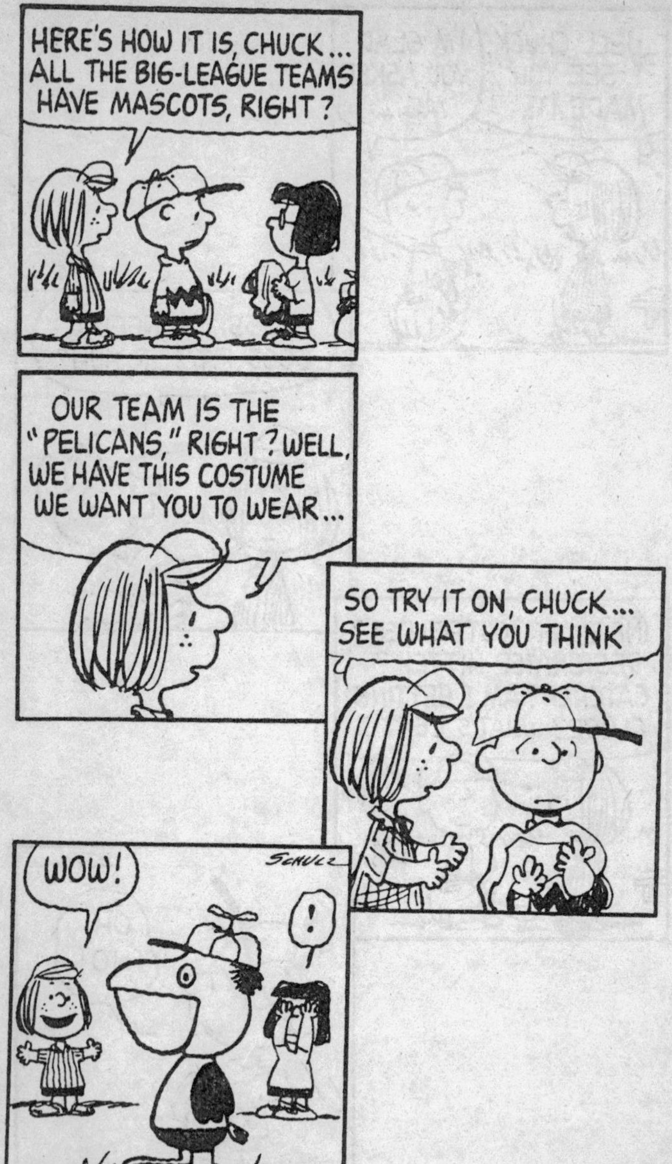
HERE'S HOW IT IS, CHUCK... ALL THE BIG-LEAGUE TEAMS HAVE MASCOTS, RIGHT?
OUR TEAM IS THE "PELICANS," RIGHT? WELL, WE HAVE THIS COSTUME WE WANT YOU TO WEAR...
SO TRY IT ON, CHUCK... SEE WHAT YOU THINK
WOW!
!
SCHULZ

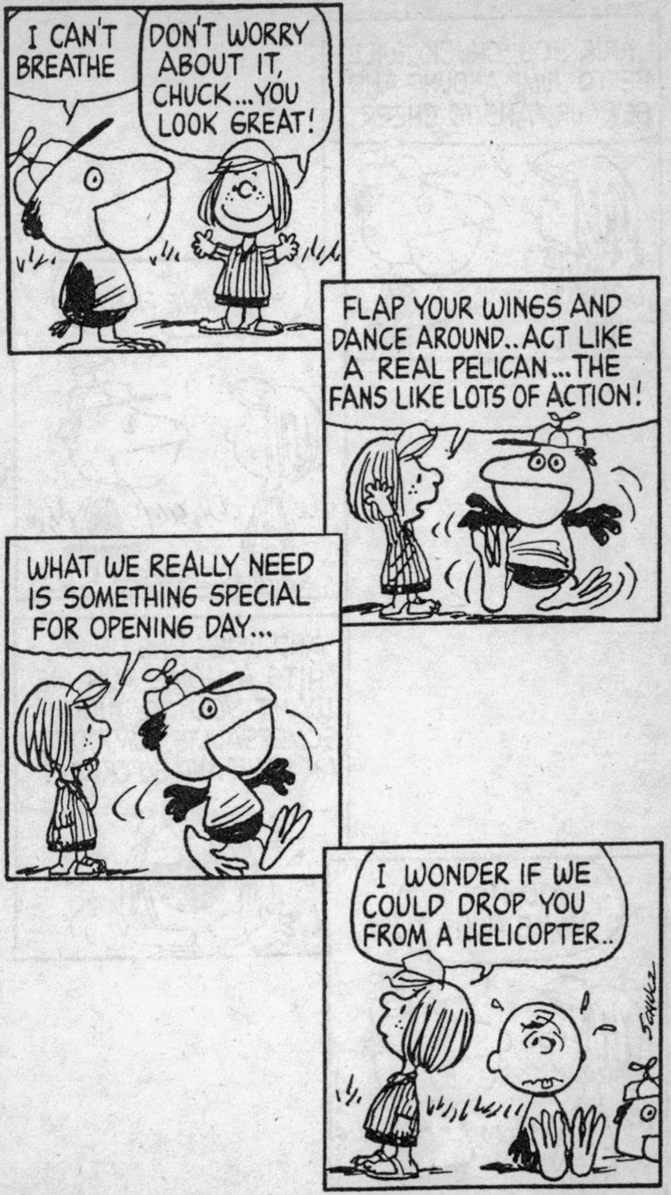
I CAN'T BREATHE
DON'T WORRY ABOUT IT, CHUCK...YOU LOOK GREAT!
FLAP YOUR WINGS AND DANCE AROUND..ACT LIKE A REAL PELICAN...THE FANS LIKE LOTS OF ACTION!
WHAT WE REALLY NEED IS SOMETHING SPECIAL FOR OPENING DAY...
I WONDER IF WE COULD DROP YOU FROM A HELICOPTER..
SCHULZ

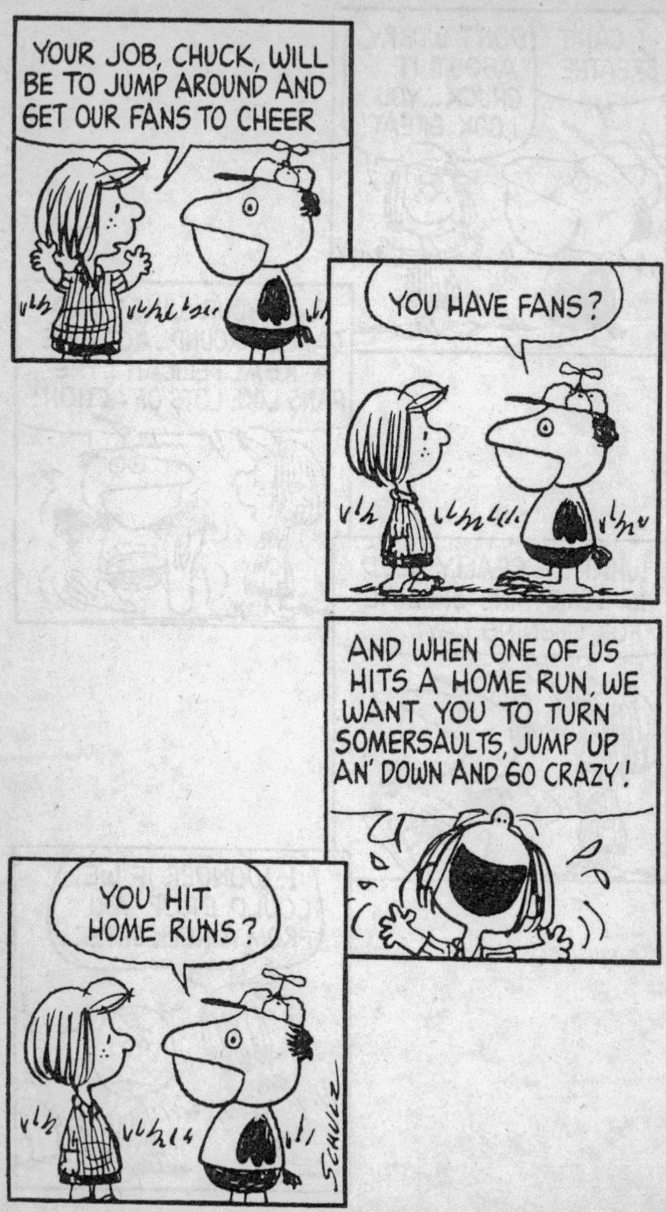
YOUR JOB, CHUCK, WILL BE TO JUMP AROUND AND GET OUR FANS TO CHEER
YOU HAVE FANS?
AND WHEN ONE OF US HITS A HOME RUN, WE WANT YOU TO TURN SOMERSAULTS, JUMP UP AN' DOWN AND GO CRAZY!
YOU HIT HOME RUNS?
SCHULZ

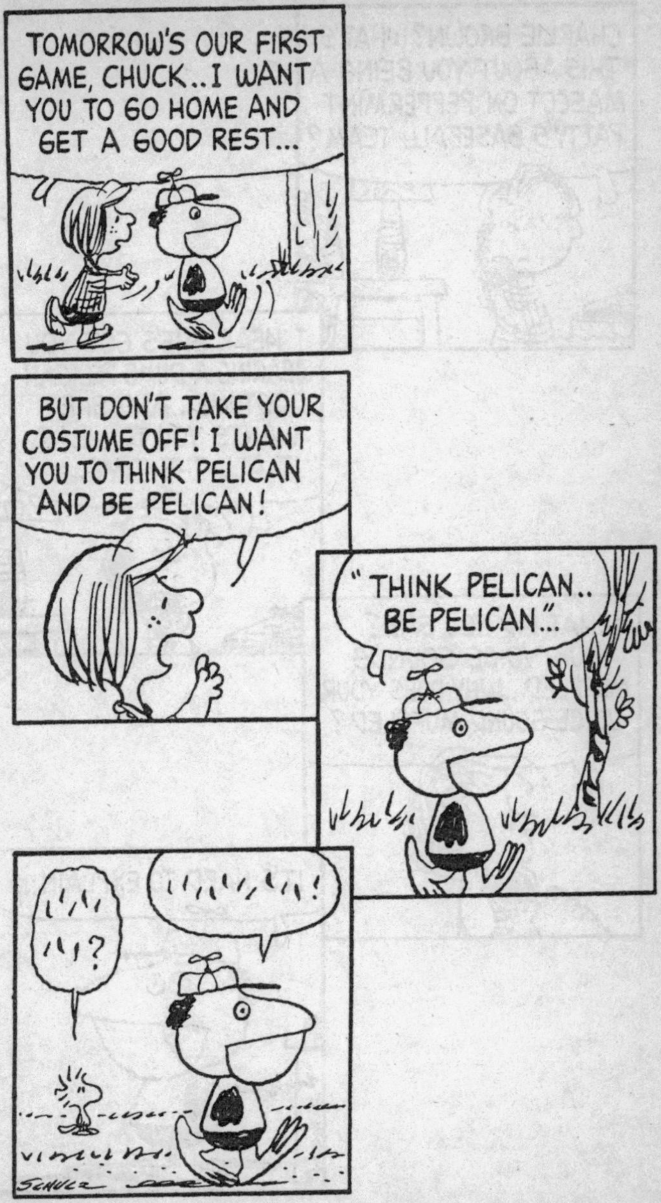
TOMORROW'S OUR FIRST GAME, CHUCK..I WANT YOU TO GO HOME AND GET A GOOD REST...
BUT DON'T TAKE YOUR COSTUME OFF! I WANT YOU TO THINK PELICAN AND BE PELICAN!
"THINK PELICAN.. BE PELICAN."...
SCHULZ

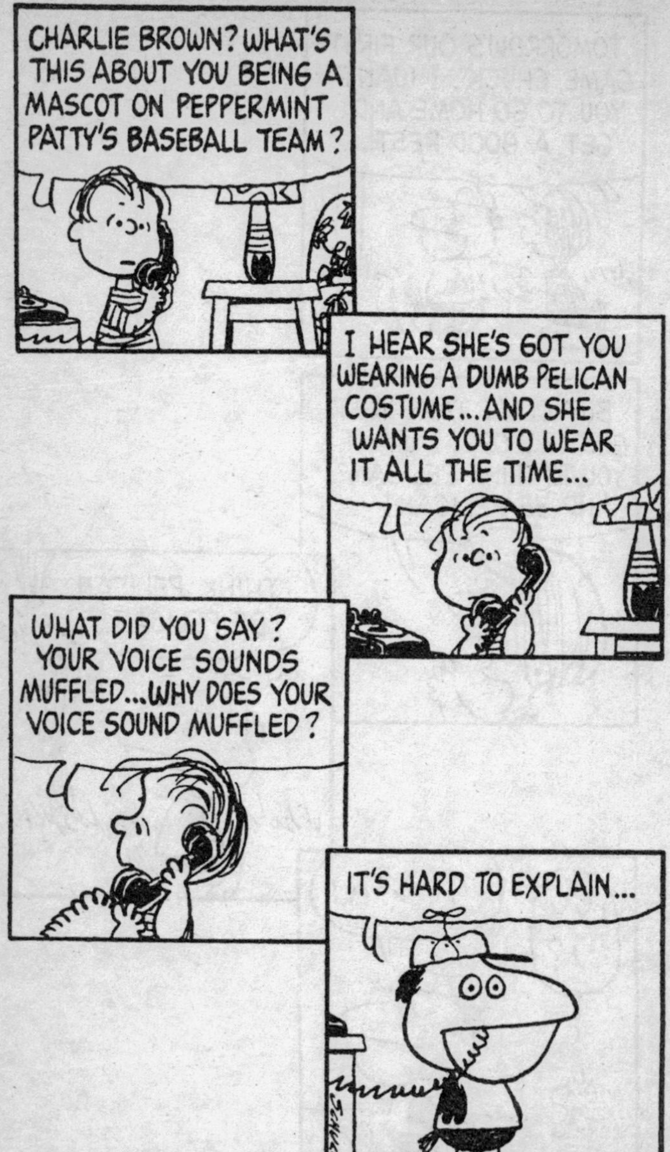
CHARLIE BROWN? WHAT'S THIS ABOUT YOU BEING A MASCOT ON PEPPERMINT PATTY'S BASEBALL TEAM?
I HEAR SHE'S GOT YOU WEARING A DUMB PELICAN COSTUME...AND SHE WANTS YOU TO WEAR IT ALL THE TIME...
WHAT DID YOU SAY? YOUR VOICE SOUNDS MUFFLED...WHY DOES YOUR VOICE SOUND MUFFLED?
IT'S HARD TO EXPLAIN...
SCHULZ

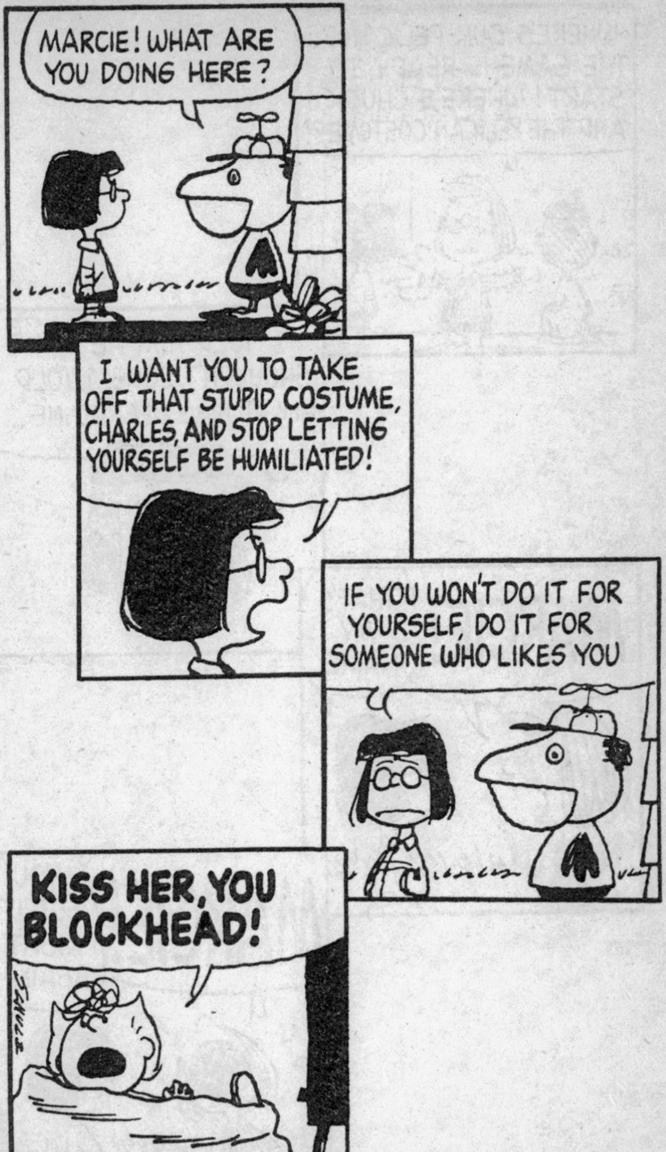
MARCIE! WHAT ARE YOU DOING HERE?
I WANT YOU TO TAKE OFF THAT STUPID COSTUME, CHARLES, AND STOP LETTING YOURSELF BE HUMILIATED!
IF YOU WON'T DO IT FOR YOURSELF, DO IT FOR SOMEONE WHO LIKES YOU
KISS HER, YOU BLOCKHEAD!
SCHULZ

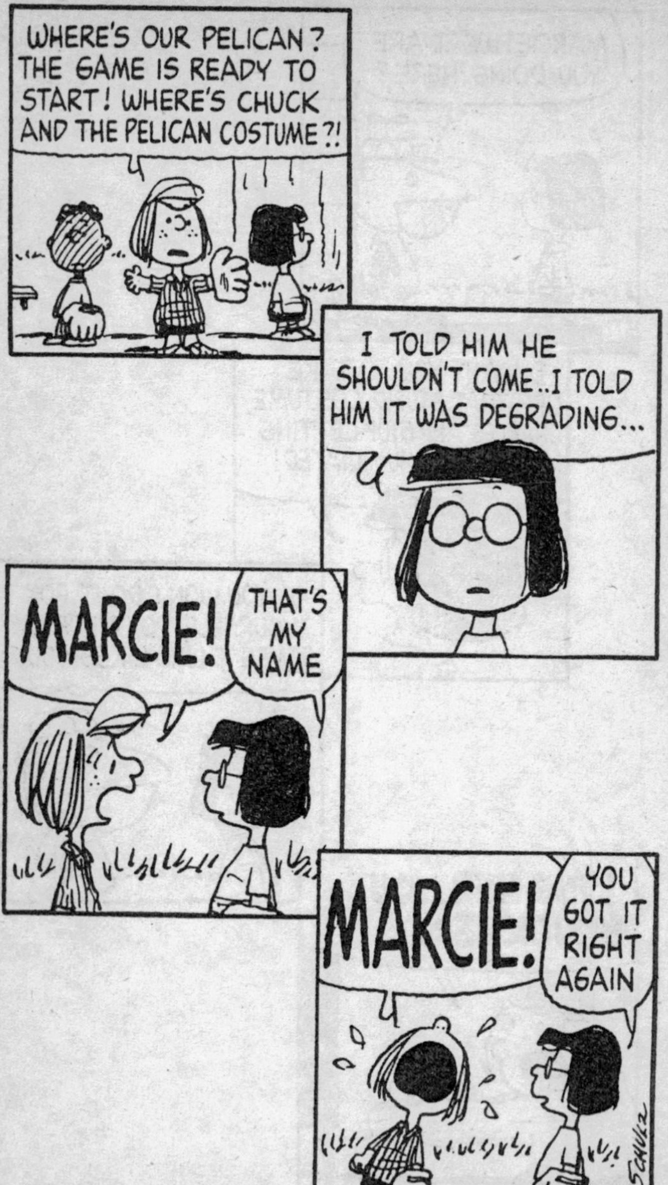
WHERE'S OUR PELICAN? THE GAME IS READY TO START! WHERE'S CHUCK AND THE PELICAN COSTUME?!
I TOLD HIM HE SHOULDN'T COME..I TOLD HIM IT WAS DEGRADING...
MARCIE!
THAT'S MY NAME
MARCIE!
YOU GOT IT RIGHT AGAIN
SCHULZ

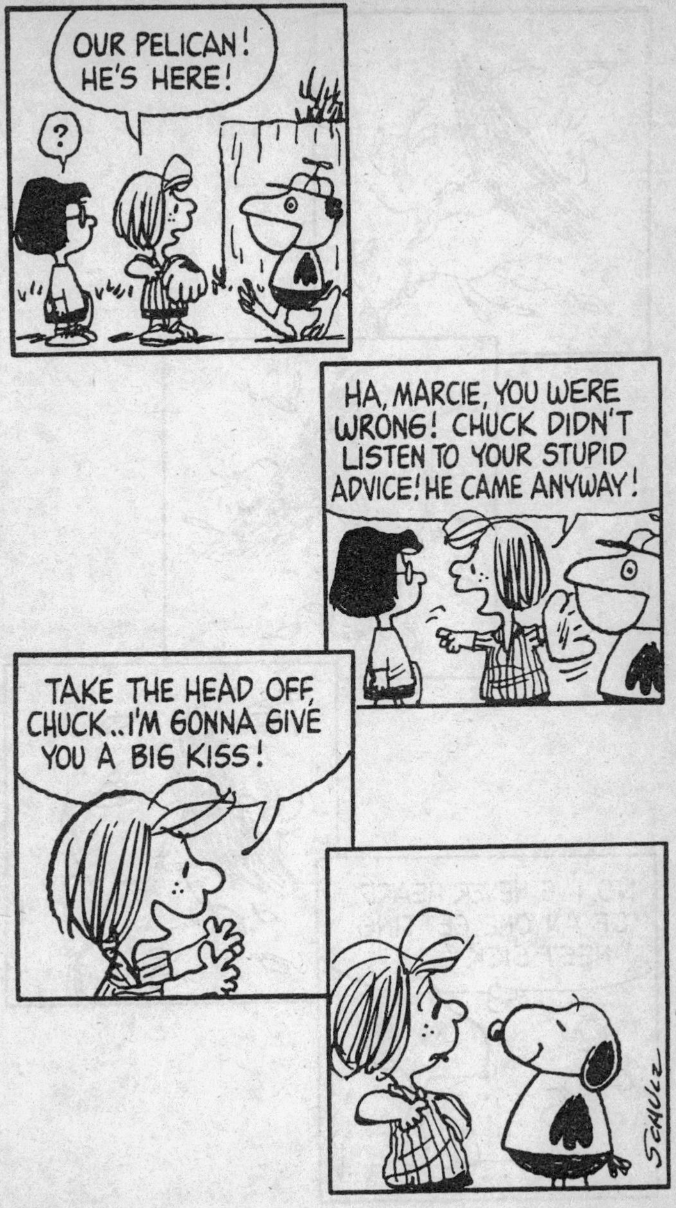
?
OUR PELICAN! HE'S HERE!
HA, MARCIE, YOU WERE WRONG! CHUCK DIDN'T LISTEN TO YOUR STUPID ADVICE! HE CAME ANYWAY!
TAKE THE HEAD OFF, CHUCK..I'M GONNA GIVE YOU A BIG KISS!
SCHULZ

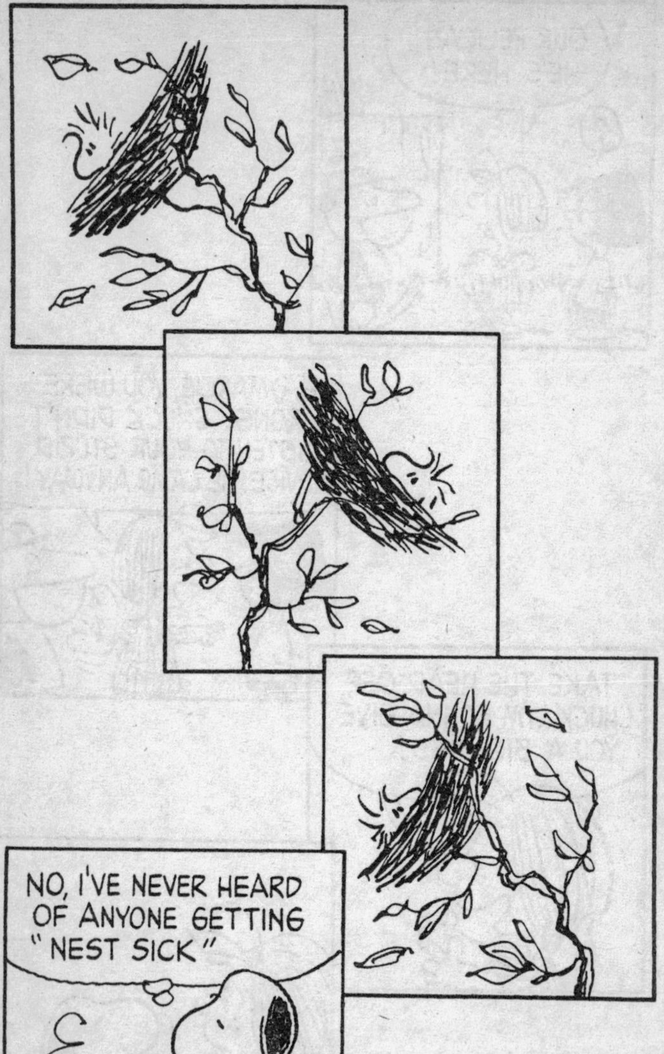
NO, I'VE NEVER HEARD OF ANYONE GETTING "NEST SICK"
SCHULZ

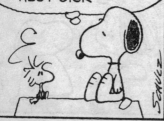

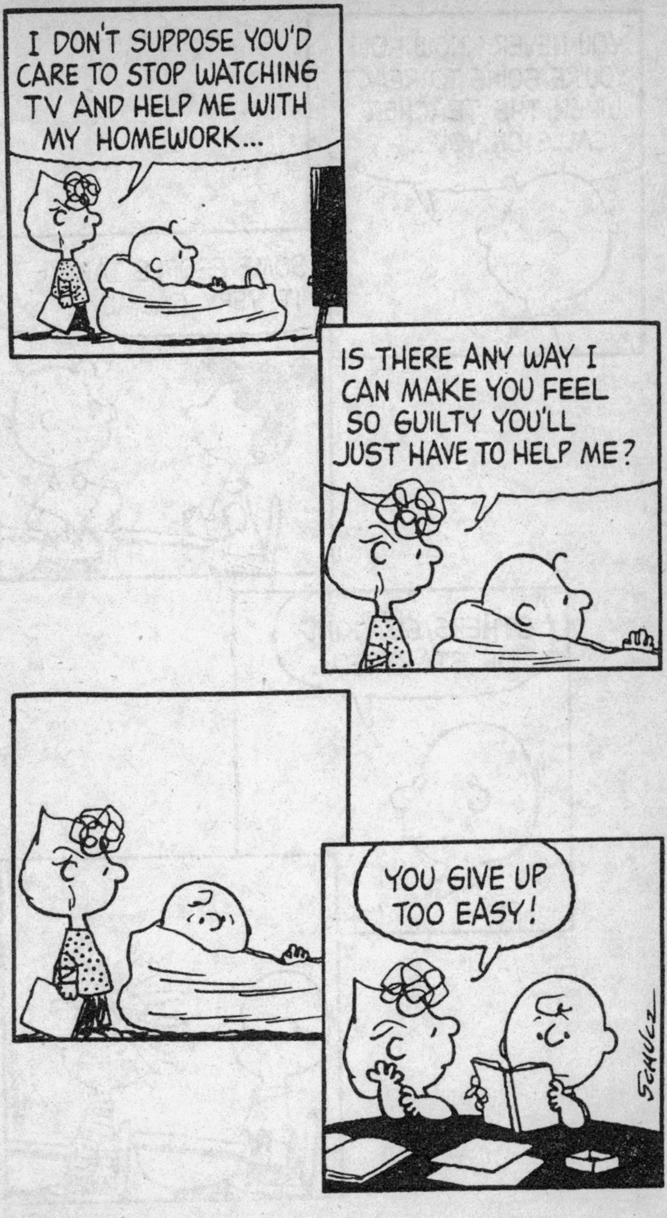
I DON'T SUPPOSE YOU'D CARE TO STOP WATCHING TV AND HELP ME WITH MY HOMEWORK...
IS THERE ANY WAY I CAN MAKE YOU FEEL SO GUILTY YOU'LL JUST HAVE TO HELP ME?
YOU GIVE UP TOO EASY!
SCHULZ

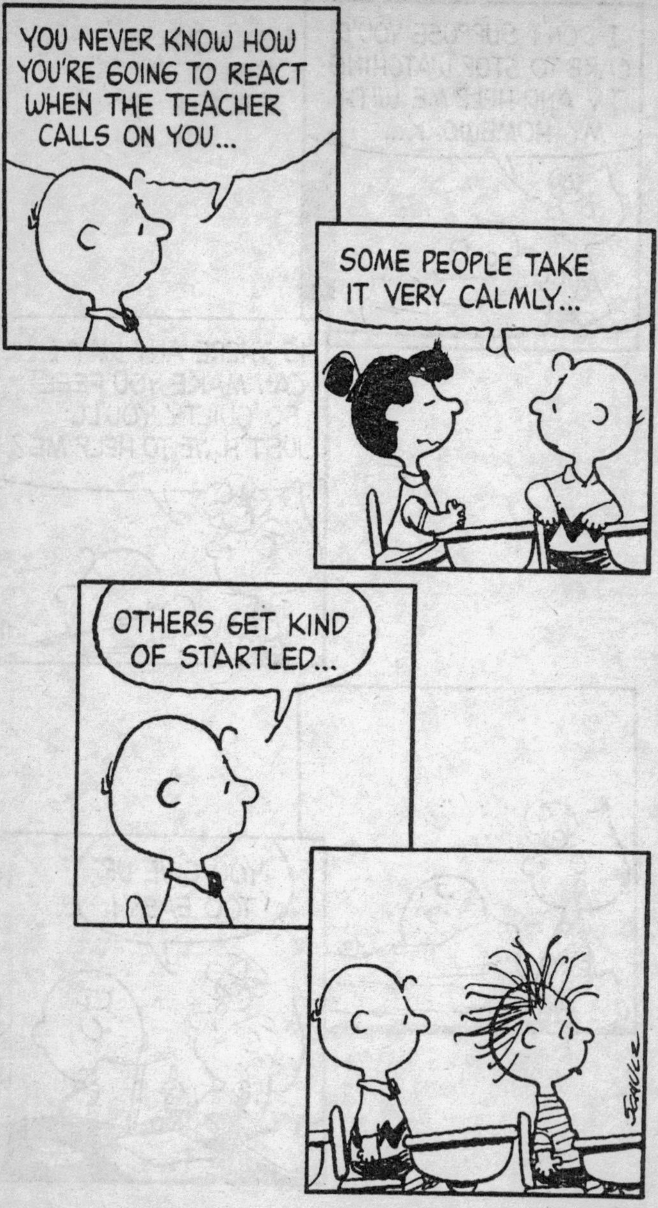
YOU NEVER KNOW HOW YOU'RE GOING TO REACT WHEN THE TEACHER CALLS ON YOU...
SOME PEOPLE TAKE IT VERY CALMLY...
OTHERS GET KIND OF STARTLED...
SCHULZ

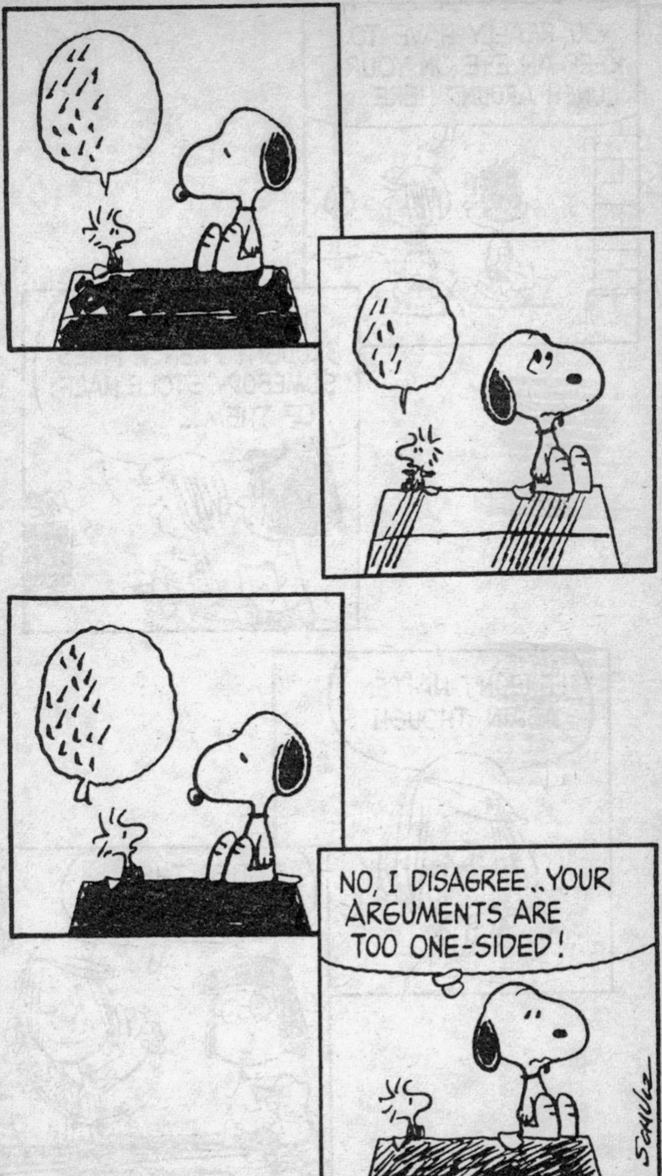
NO, I DISAGREE..YOUR ARGUMENTS ARE TOO ONE-SIDED!
SCHULZ

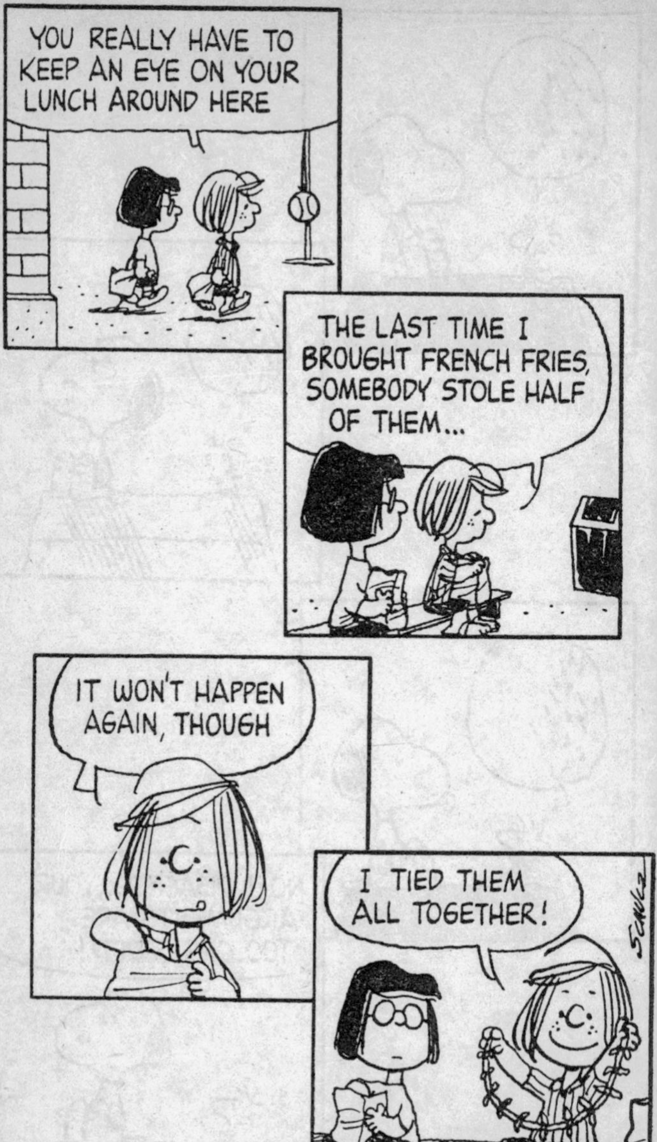
YOU REALLY HAVE TO KEEP AN EYE ON YOUR LUNCH AROUND HERE
THE LAST TIME I BROUGHT FRENCH FRIES, SOMEBODY STOLE HALF OF THEM...
IT WON'T HAPPEN AGAIN, THOUGH
I TIED THEM ALL TOGETHER!
SCHULZ

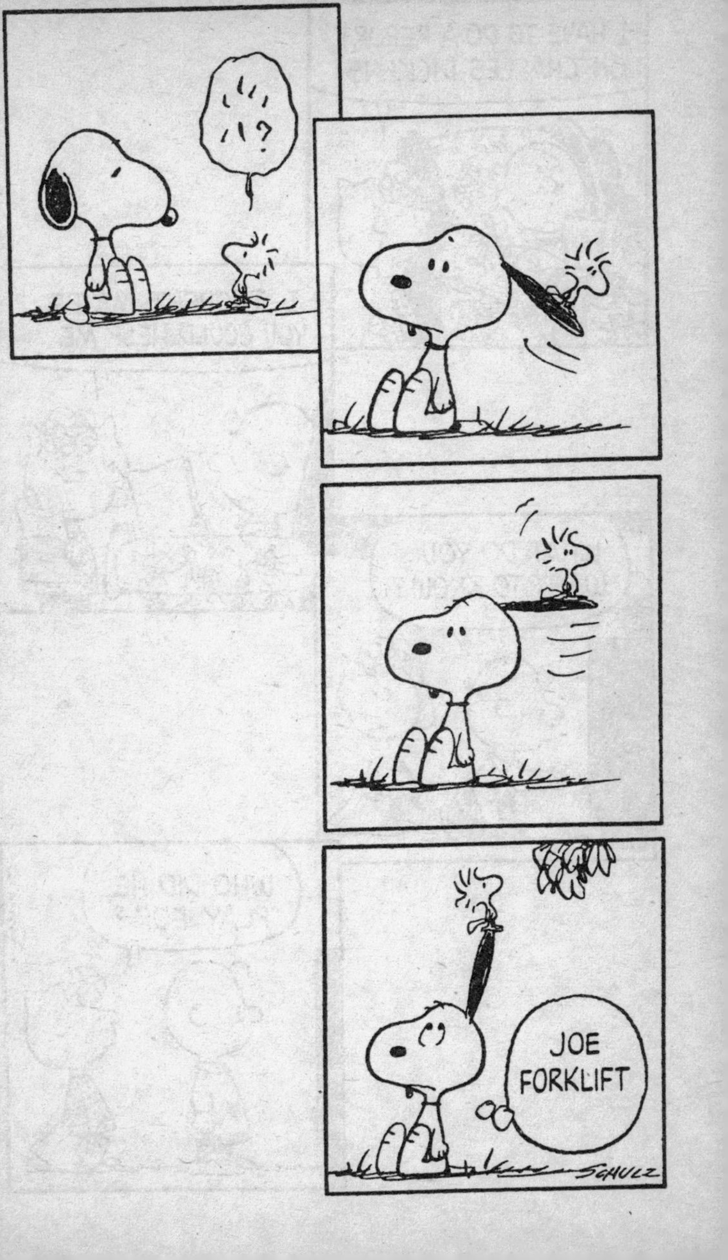
JOE
FORKLIFT
SCHULZ

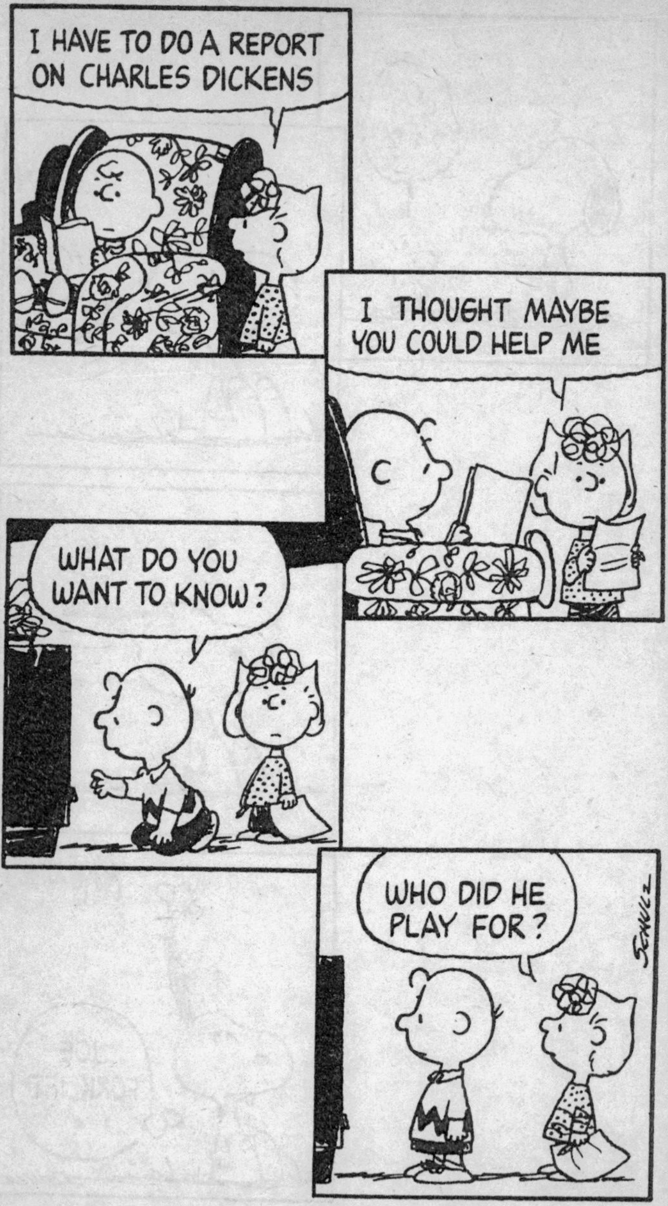
I HAVE TO DO A REPORT ON CHARLES DICKENS
I THOUGHT MAYBE YOU COULD HELP ME
WHAT DO YOU WANT TO KNOW?
WHO DID HE PLAY FOR?
SCHULZ

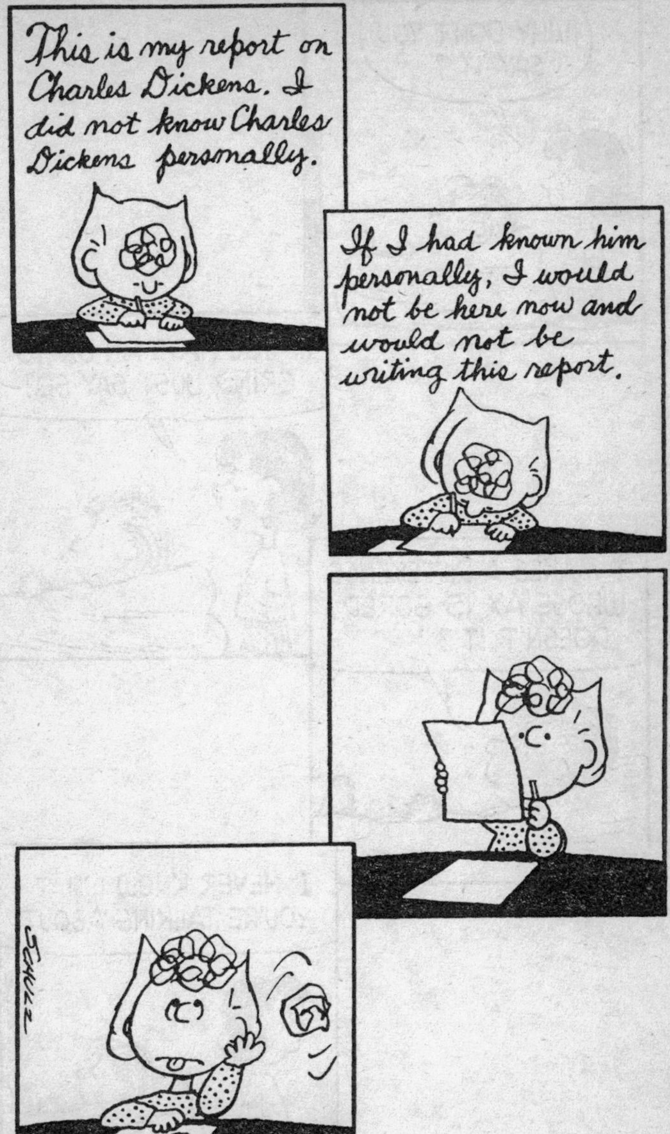
This is my report on Charles Dickens. I did not know Charles Dickens personally.
If I had known him personally, I would not be here now and would not be writing this report.
SCHULZ

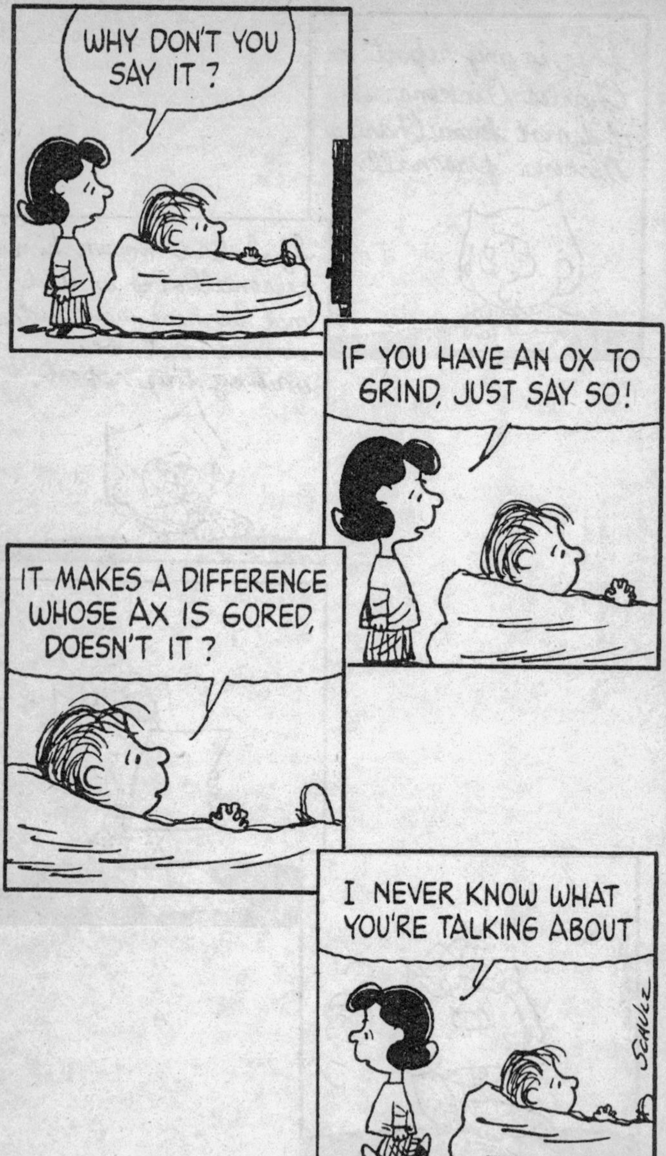
WHY DON'T YOU SAY IT ?
IF YOU HAVE AN OX TO GRIND, JUST SAY SO!
IT MAKES A DIFFERENCE WHOSE AX IS GORED, DOESN'T IT ?
I NEVER KNOW WHAT YOU'RE TALKING ABOUT
SCHULZ

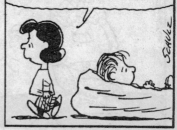

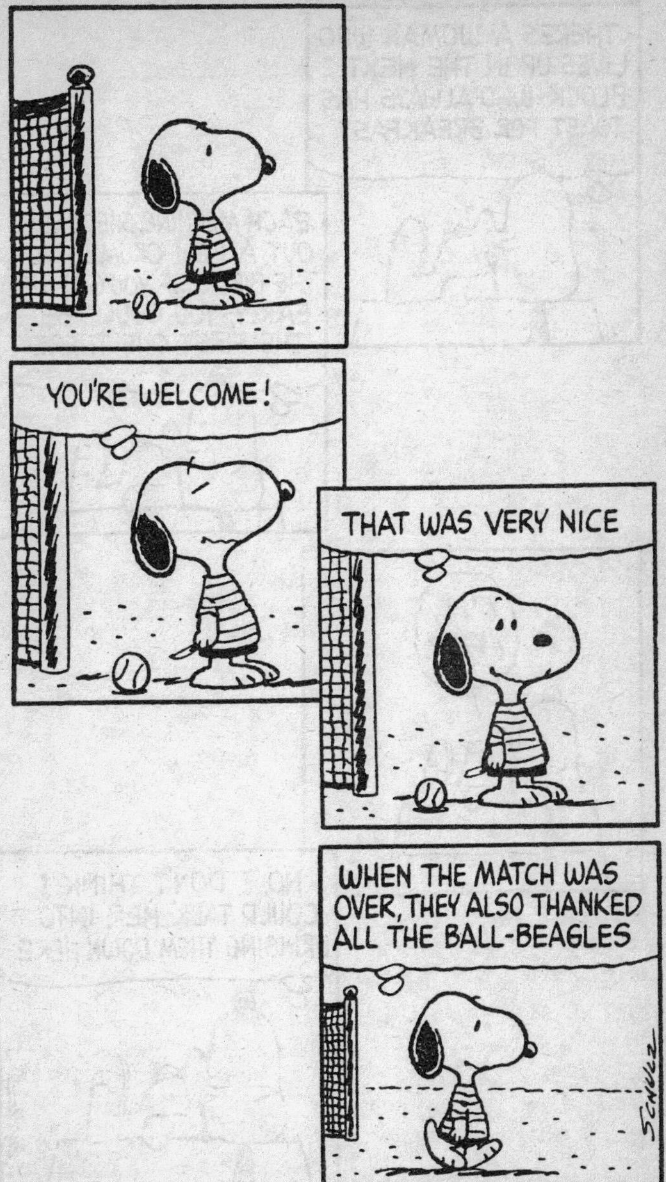
YOU'RE WELCOME!
THAT WAS VERY NICE
WHEN THE MATCH WAS OVER, THEY ALSO THANKED ALL THE BALL-BEAGLES
SCHULZ

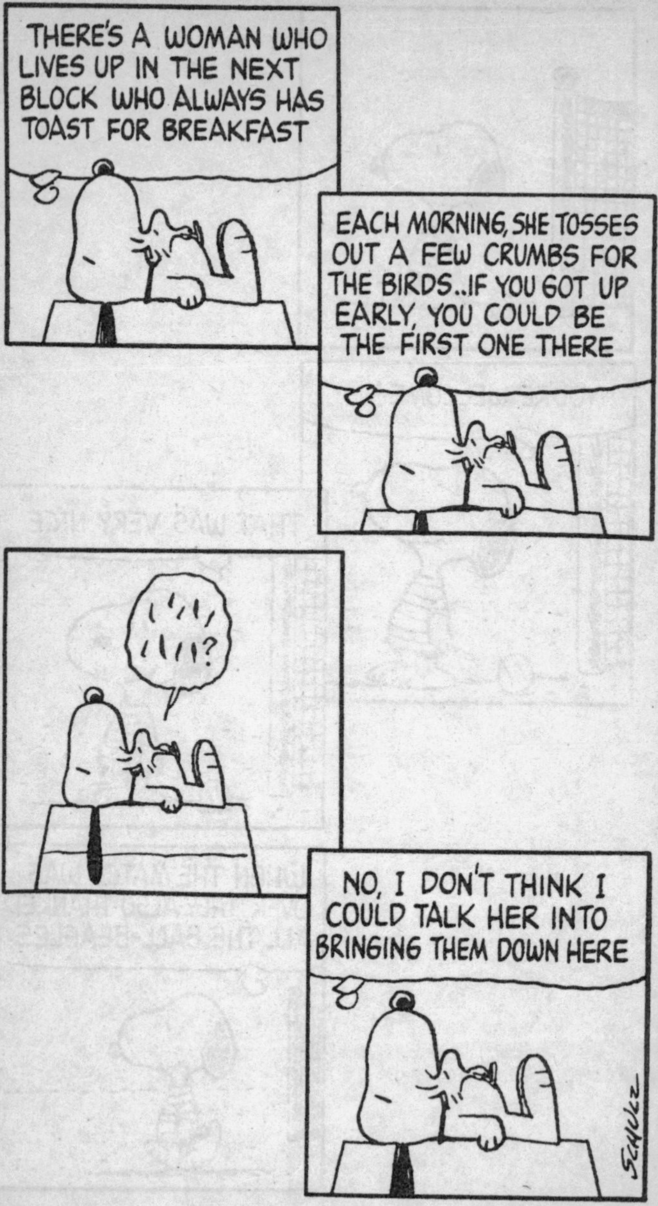
THERE'S A WOMAN WHO LIVES UP IN THE NEXT BLOCK WHO ALWAYS HAS TOAST FOR BREAKFAST
EACH MORNING, SHE TOSSES OUT A FEW CRUMBS FOR THE BIRDS..IF YOU GOT UP EARLY, YOU COULD BE THE FIRST ONE THERE
?
NO, I DON'T THINK I COULD TALK HER INTO BRINGING THEM DOWN HERE
SCHULZ

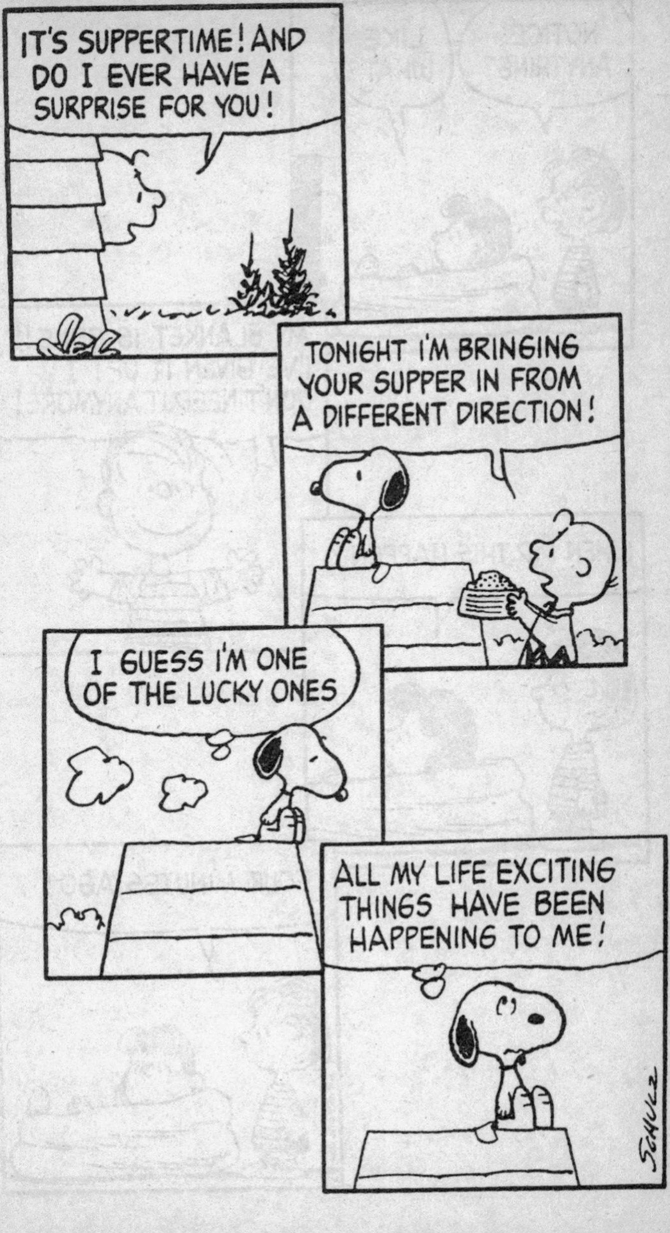
IT'S SUPPERTIME! AND DO I EVER HAVE A SURPRISE FOR YOU!
TONIGHT I'M BRINGING YOUR SUPPER IN FROM A DIFFERENT DIRECTION!
I GUESS I'M ONE OF THE LUCKY ONES
ALL MY LIFE EXCITING THINGS HAVE BEEN HAPPENING TO ME!
SCHULZ

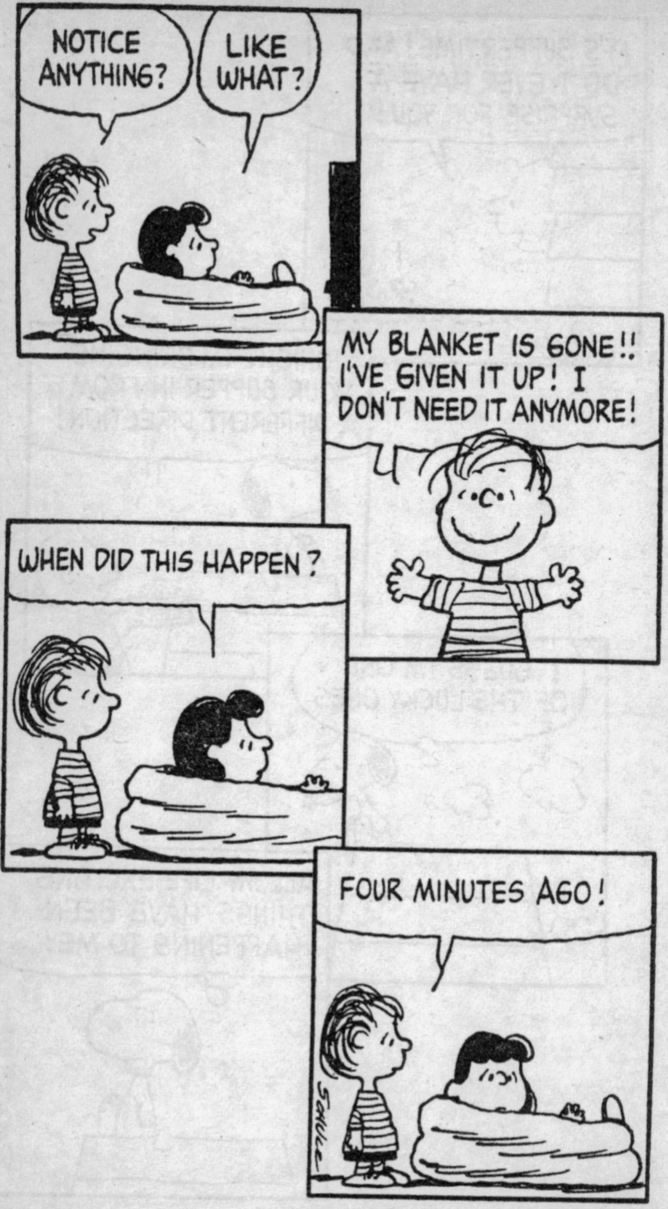
NOTICE ANYTHING?
LIKE WHAT?
MY BLANKET IS GONE!! I'VE GIVEN IT UP! I DON'T NEED IT ANYMORE!
WHEN DID THIS HAPPEN?
FOUR MINUTES AGO!
SCHULZ

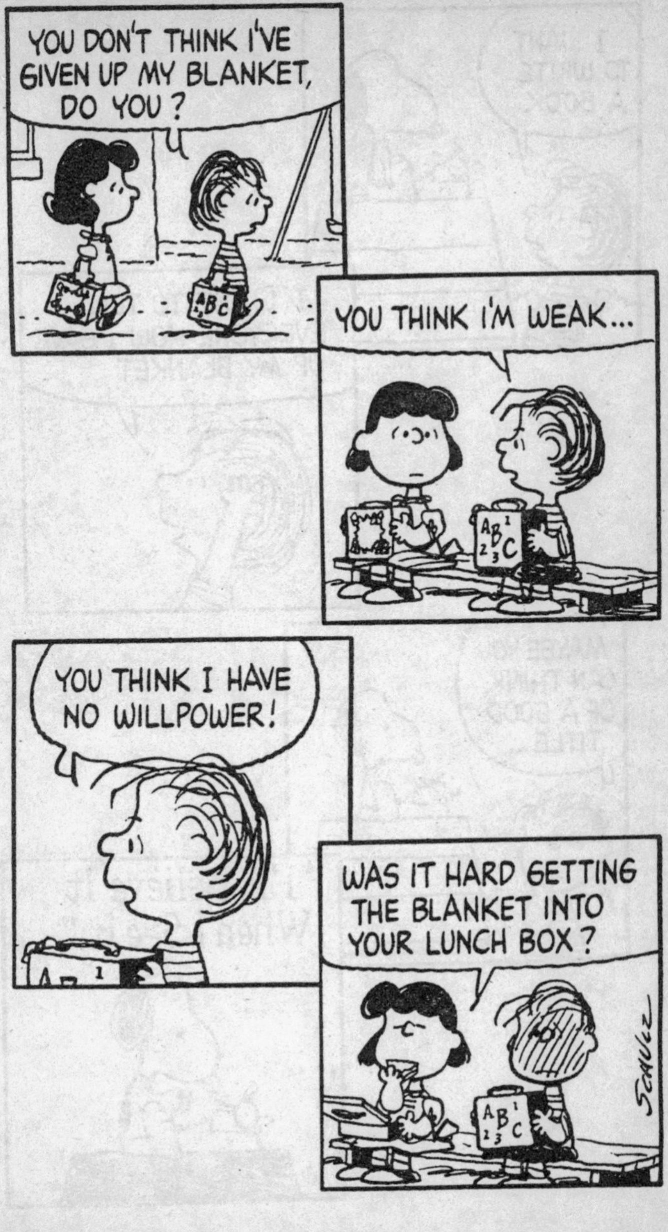
YOU DON'T THINK I'VE GIVEN UP MY BLANKET, DO YOU ?
ABC
YOU THINK I'M WEAK...
ABC 123
YOU THINK I HAVE NO WILLPOWER!
WAS IT HARD GETTING THE BLANKET INTO YOUR LUNCH BOX ?
SCHULZ

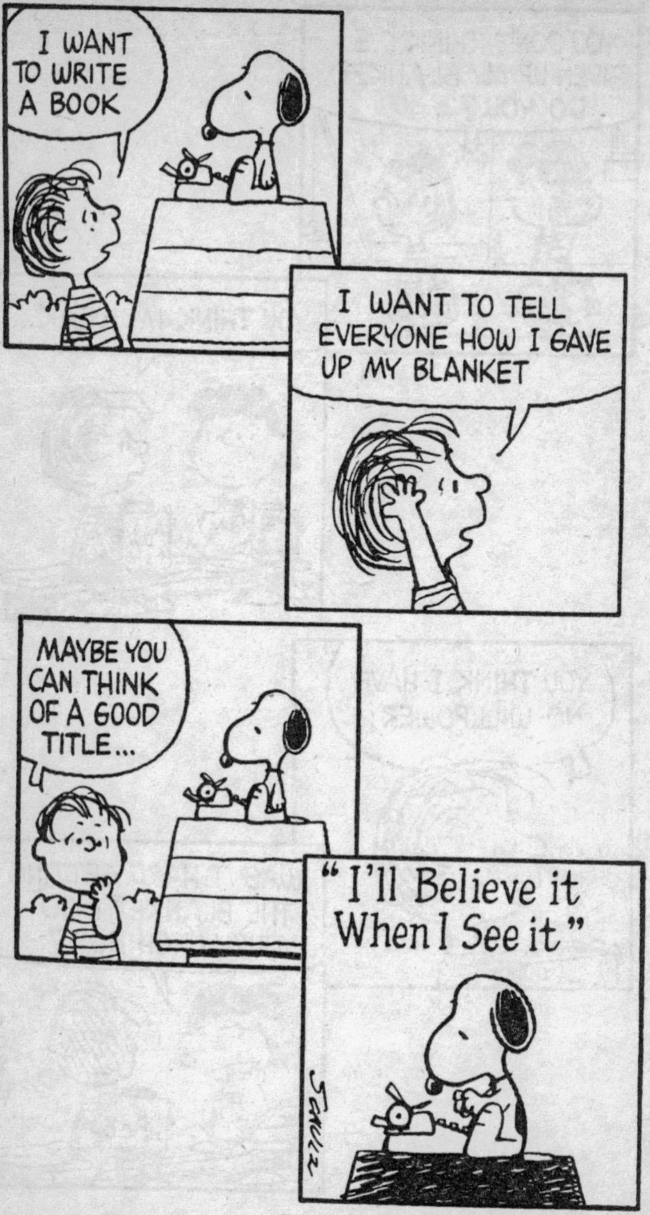
I WANT TO WRITE A BOOK
I WANT TO TELL EVERYONE HOW I GAVE UP MY BLANKET
MAYBE YOU CAN THINK OF A GOOD TITLE...
"I'll Believe it When I See it"
SCHULZ

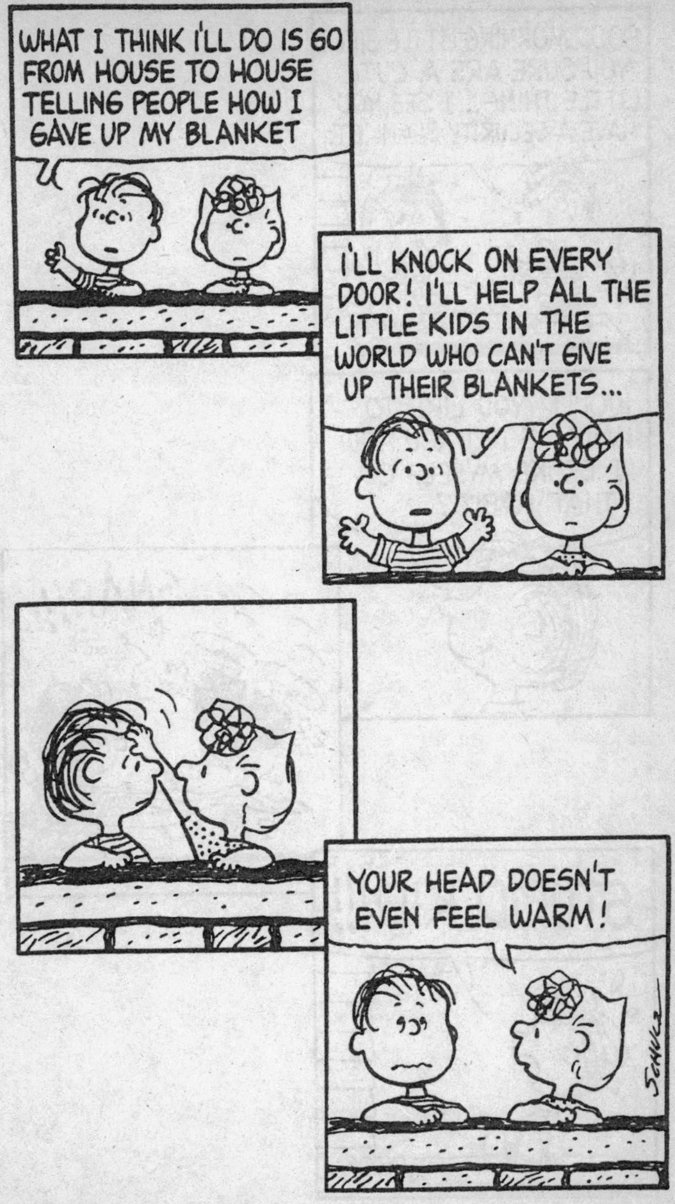
WHAT I THINK I'LL DO IS GO FROM HOUSE TO HOUSE TELLING PEOPLE HOW I GAVE UP MY BLANKET
I'LL KNOCK ON EVERY DOOR! I'LL HELP ALL THE LITTLE KIDS IN THE WORLD WHO CAN'T GIVE UP THEIR BLANKETS...
YOUR HEAD DOESN'T EVEN FEEL WARM!
SCHULZ

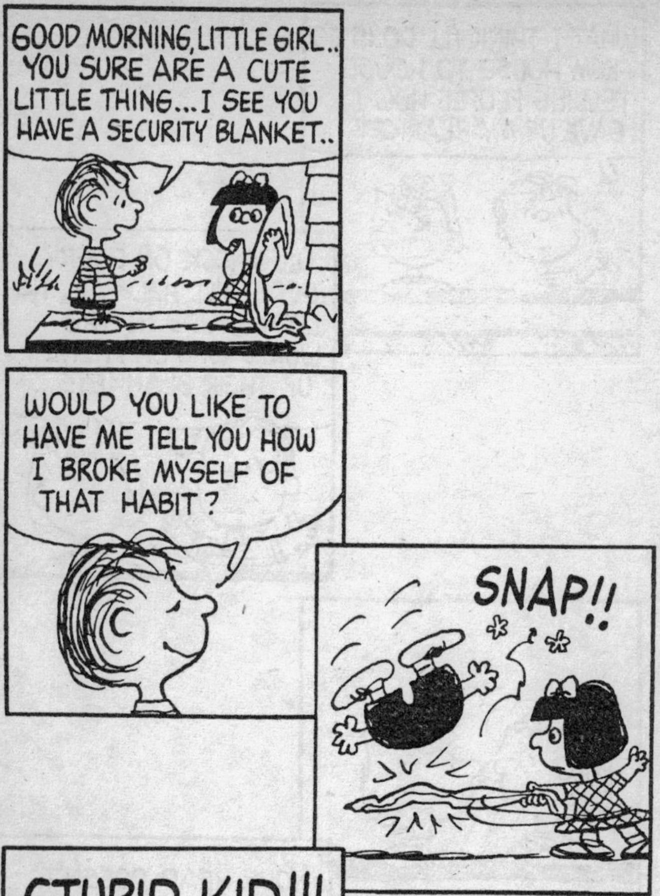
GOOD MORNING, LITTLE GIRL.. YOU SURE ARE A CUTE LITTLE THING...I SEE YOU HAVE A SECURITY BLANKET..
WOULD YOU LIKE TO HAVE ME TELL YOU HOW I BROKE MYSELF OF THAT HABIT?
SNAP!!
STUPID KID!!!

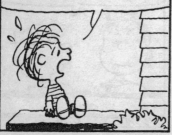

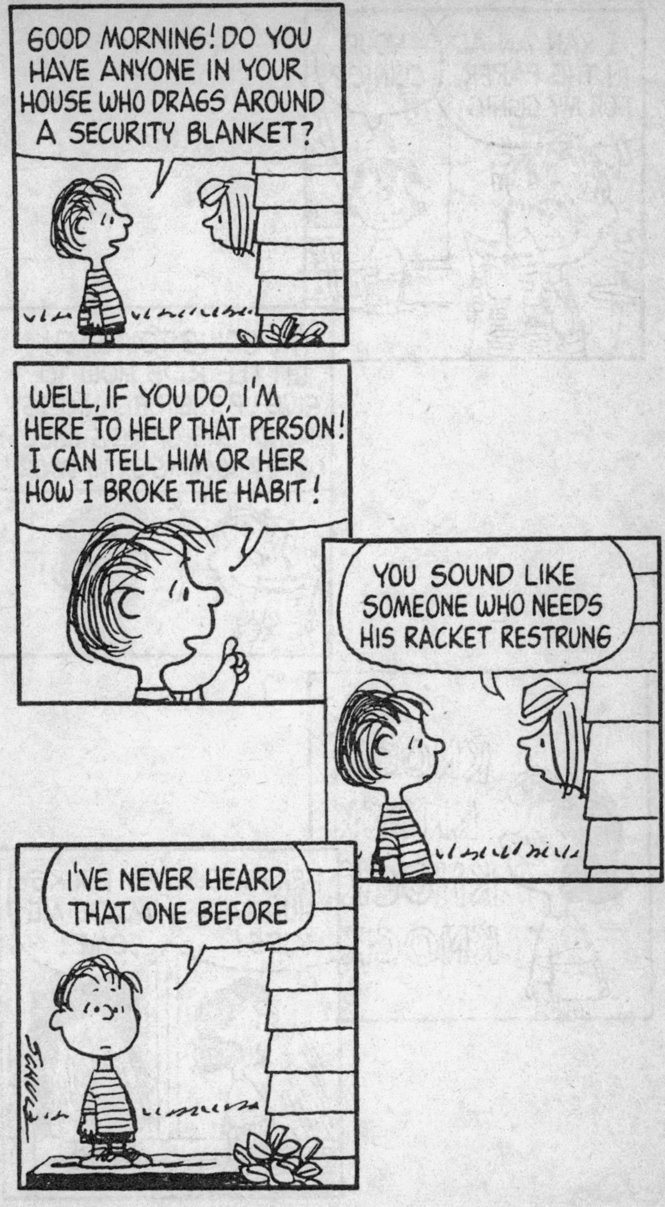
GOOD MORNING! DO YOU HAVE ANYONE IN YOUR HOUSE WHO DRAGS AROUND A SECURITY BLANKET?
WELL, IF YOU DO, I'M HERE TO HELP THAT PERSON! I CAN TELL HIM OR HER HOW I BROKE THE HABIT!
YOU SOUND LIKE SOMEONE WHO NEEDS HIS RACKET RESTRUNG
I'VE NEVER HEARD THAT ONE BEFORE
SCHULZ

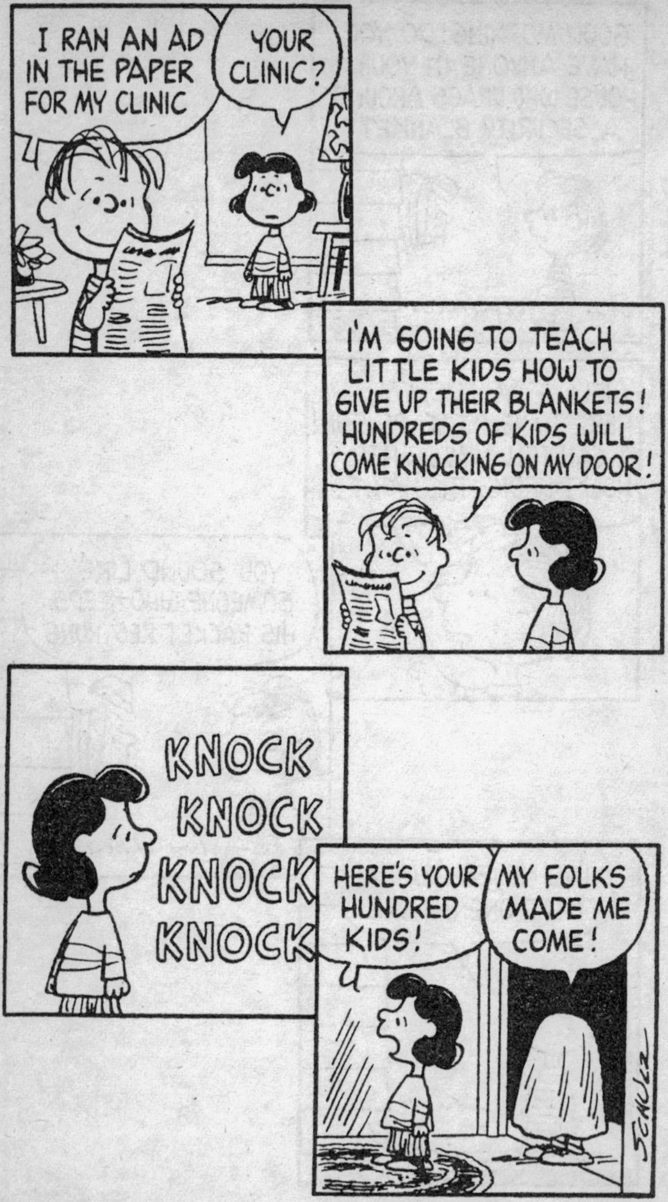
I RAN AN AD IN THE PAPER FOR MY CLINIC
YOUR CLINIC?
I'M GOING TO TEACH LITTLE KIDS HOW TO GIVE UP THEIR BLANKETS! HUNDREDS OF KIDS WILL COME KNOCKING ON MY DOOR!
KNOCK KNOCK KNOCK KNOCK
HERE'S YOUR HUNDRED KIDS!
MY FOLKS MADE ME COME!
SCHULZ

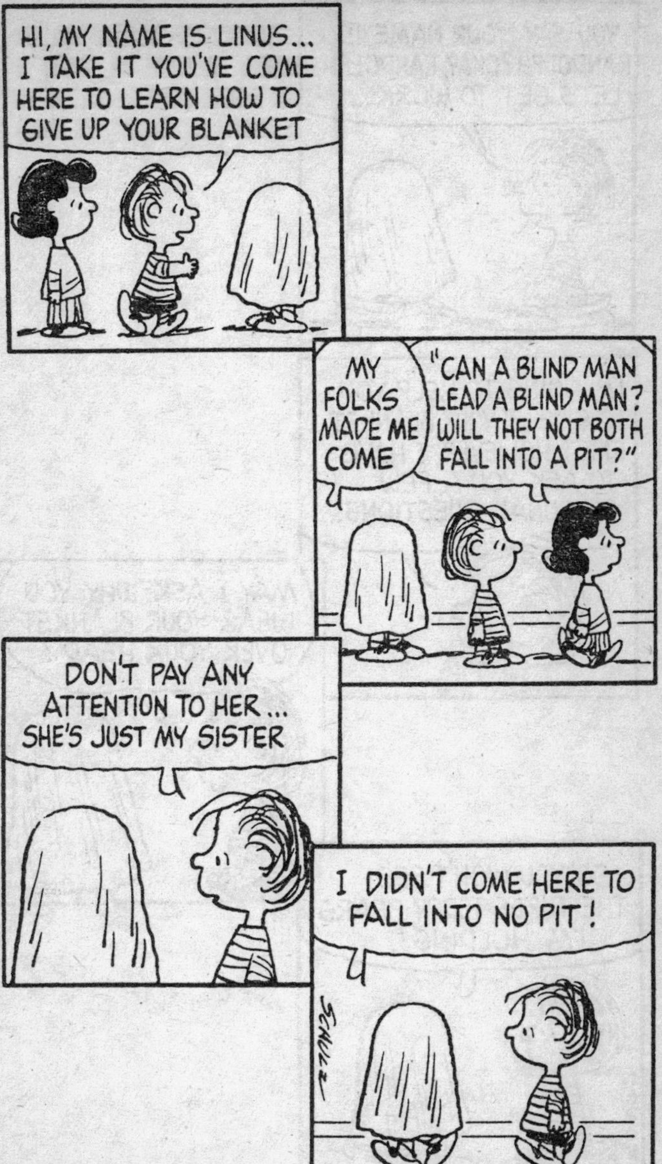
HI, MY NAME IS LINUS... I TAKE IT YOU'VE COME HERE TO LEARN HOW TO GIVE UP YOUR BLANKET
MY FOLKS MADE ME COME
"CAN A BLIND MAN LEAD A BLIND MAN? WILL THEY NOT BOTH FALL INTO A PIT?"
DON'T PAY ANY ATTENTION TO HER... SHE'S JUST MY SISTER
I DIDN'T COME HERE TO FALL INTO NO PIT!
SCHULZ

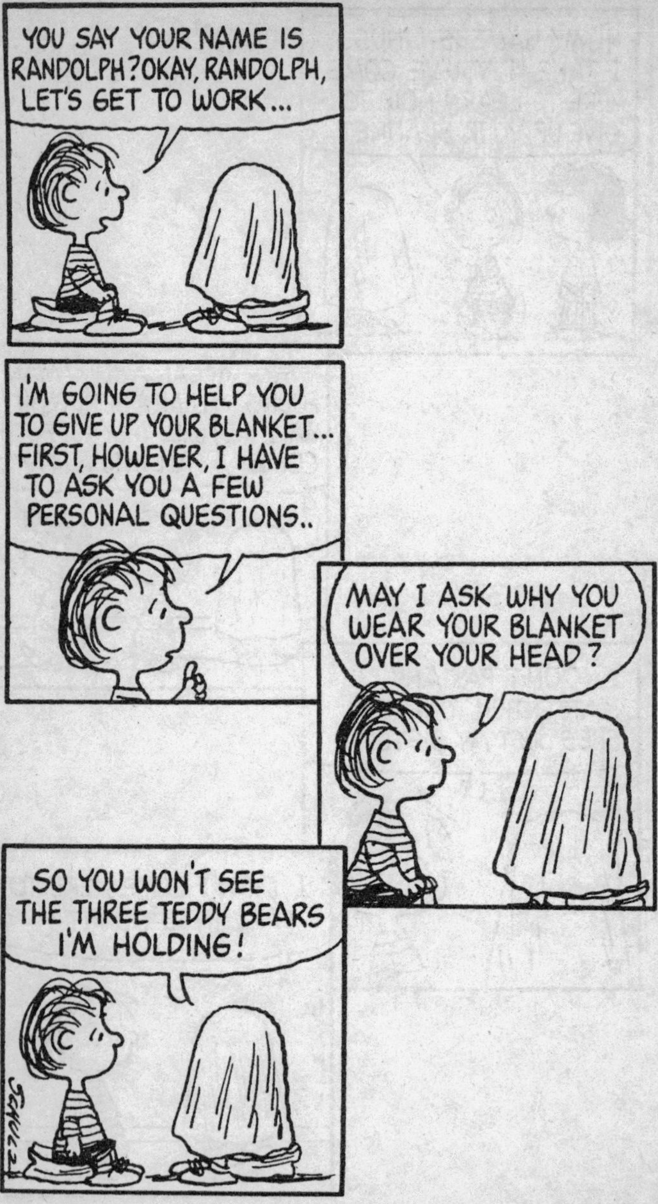
YOU SAY YOUR NAME IS RANDOLPH? OKAY, RANDOLPH, LET'S GET TO WORK...
I'M GOING TO HELP YOU TO GIVE UP YOUR BLANKET... FIRST, HOWEVER, I HAVE TO ASK YOU A FEW PERSONAL QUESTIONS..
MAY I ASK WHY YOU WEAR YOUR BLANKET OVER YOUR HEAD?
SO YOU WON'T SEE THE THREE TEDDY BEARS I'M HOLDING!

I THINK THE FIRST THING WE SHOULD CONSIDER ABOUT CLINGING TO A SECURITY BLANKET IS GUILT
I DON'T FEEL GUILTY
GOOD! NOW, THERE'S ALSO EMBARRASSMENT
THAT'S NO PROBLEM, EITHER
NOW MENTION STUPIDITY!
SCHULZ

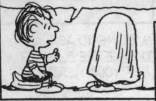

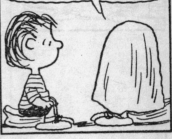

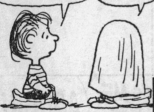

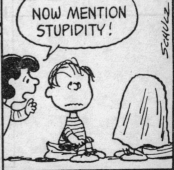

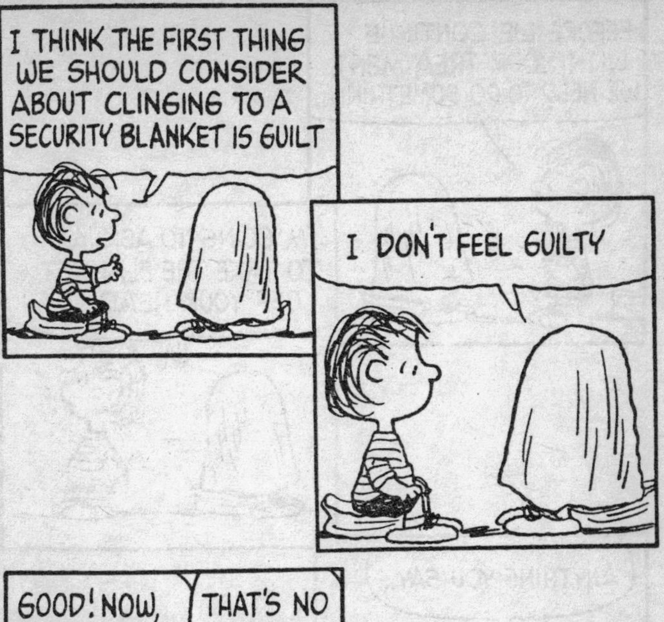

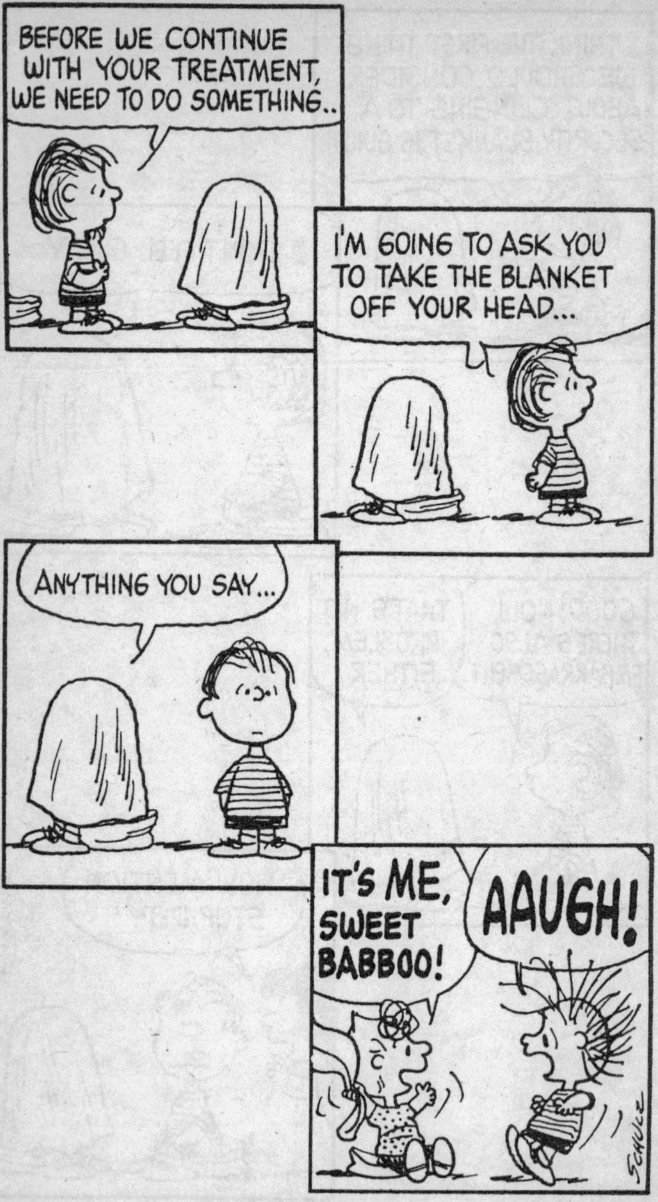
BEFORE WE CONTINUE WITH YOUR TREATMENT, WE NEED TO DO SOMETHING..
I'M GOING TO ASK YOU TO TAKE THE BLANKET OFF YOUR HEAD...
ANYTHING YOU SAY...
IT'S ME, SWEET BABBOO!
AAUGH!
SCHULZ

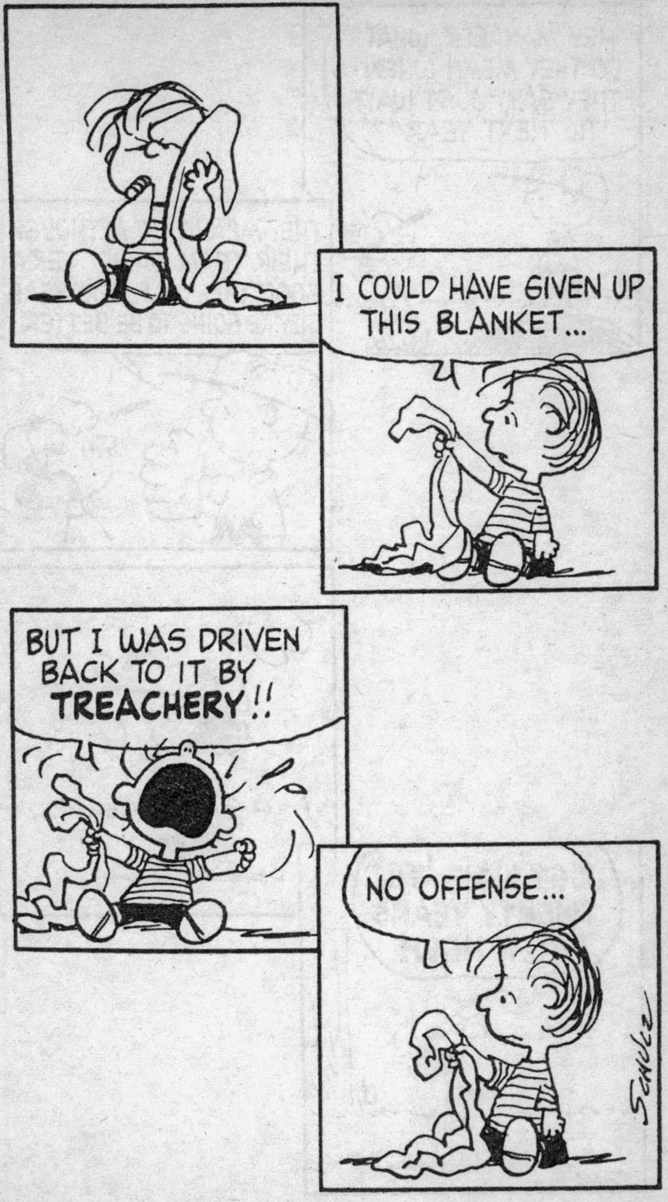
I COULD HAVE GIVEN UP THIS BLANKET...
BUT I WAS DRIVEN BACK TO IT BY TREACHERY!!
NO OFFENSE...
SCHULZ

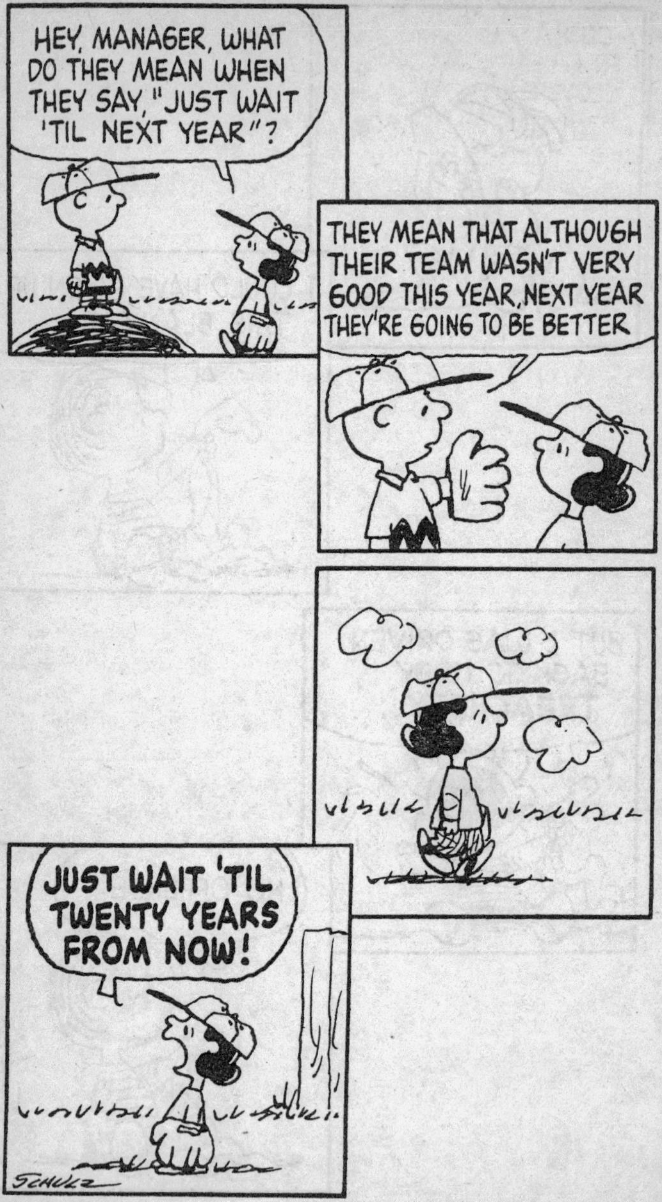
HEY, MANAGER, WHAT DO THEY MEAN WHEN THEY SAY, "JUST WAIT 'TIL NEXT YEAR"?
THEY MEAN THAT ALTHOUGH THEIR TEAM WASN'T VERY GOOD THIS YEAR, NEXT YEAR THEY'RE GOING TO BE BETTER
JUST WAIT 'TIL TWENTY YEARS FROM NOW!
SCHULZ

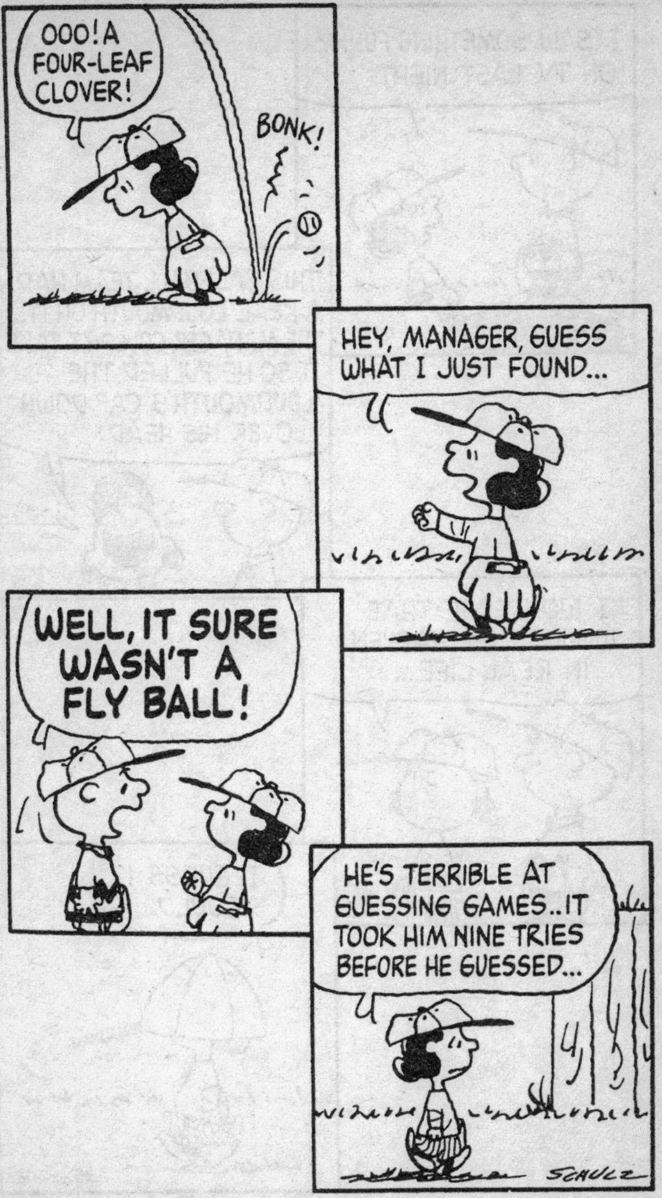
OOO! A FOUR-LEAF CLOVER!
BONK!
HEY, MANAGER, GUESS WHAT I JUST FOUND...
WELL, IT SURE WASN'T A FLY BALL!
HE'S TERRIBLE AT GUESSING GAMES..IT TOOK HIM NINE TRIES BEFORE HE GUESSED...
SCHULZ

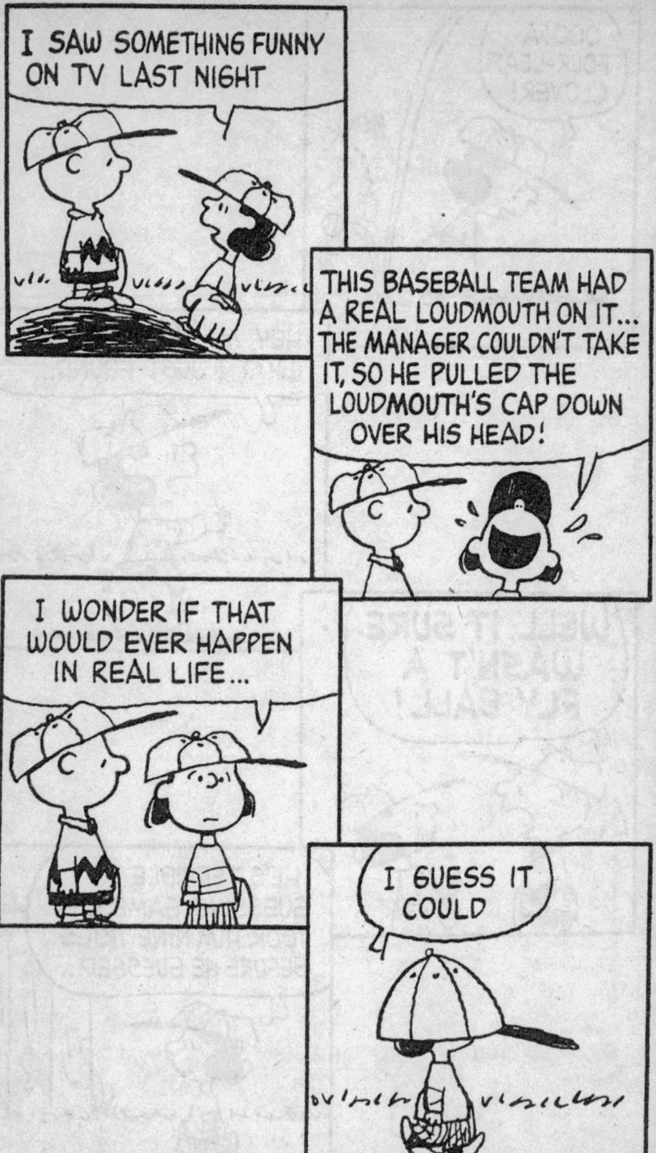
I SAW SOMETHING FUNNY ON TV LAST NIGHT
THIS BASEBALL TEAM HAD A REAL LOUDMOUTH ON IT... THE MANAGER COULDN'T TAKE IT, SO HE PULLED THE LOUDMOUTH'S CAP DOWN OVER HIS HEAD!
I WONDER IF THAT WOULD EVER HAPPEN IN REAL LIFE...
I GUESS IT COULD
SCHULZ

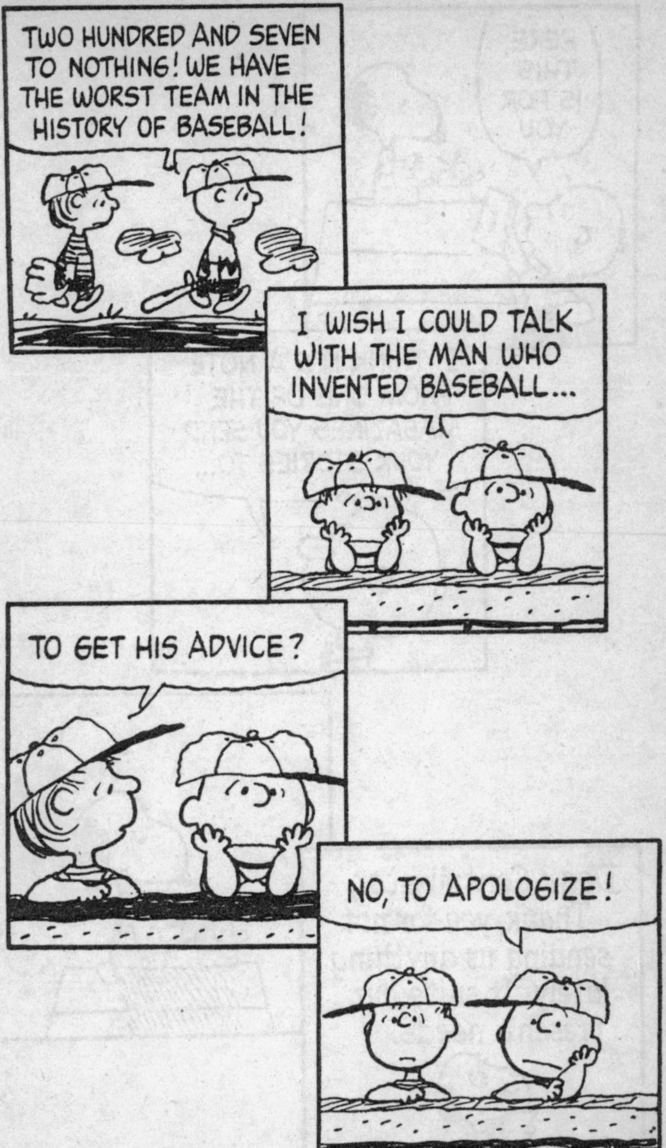
TWO HUNDRED AND SEVEN TO NOTHING! WE HAVE THE WORST TEAM IN THE HISTORY OF BASEBALL!
I WISH I COULD TALK WITH THE MAN WHO INVENTED BASEBALL...
TO GET HIS ADVICE?
NO, TO APOLOGIZE!
SCHULZ

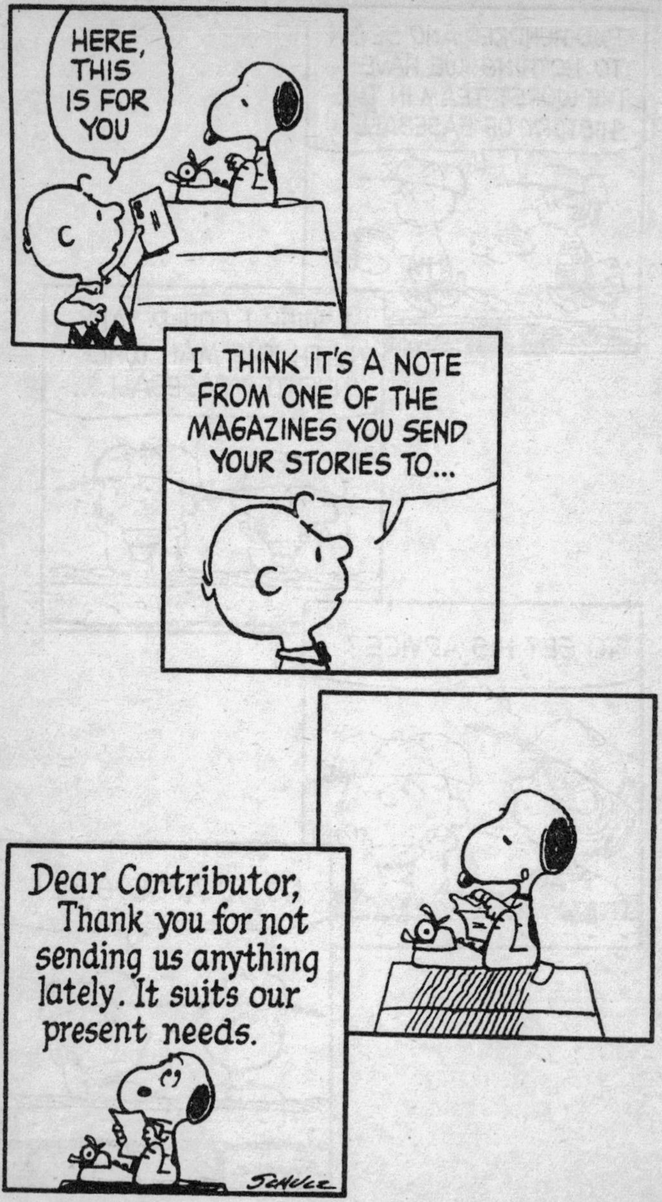
HERE, THIS IS FOR YOU
I THINK IT'S A NOTE FROM ONE OF THE MAGAZINES YOU SEND YOUR STORIES TO...
Dear Contributor,
Thank you for not sending us anything lately. It suits our present needs.
SCHULZ

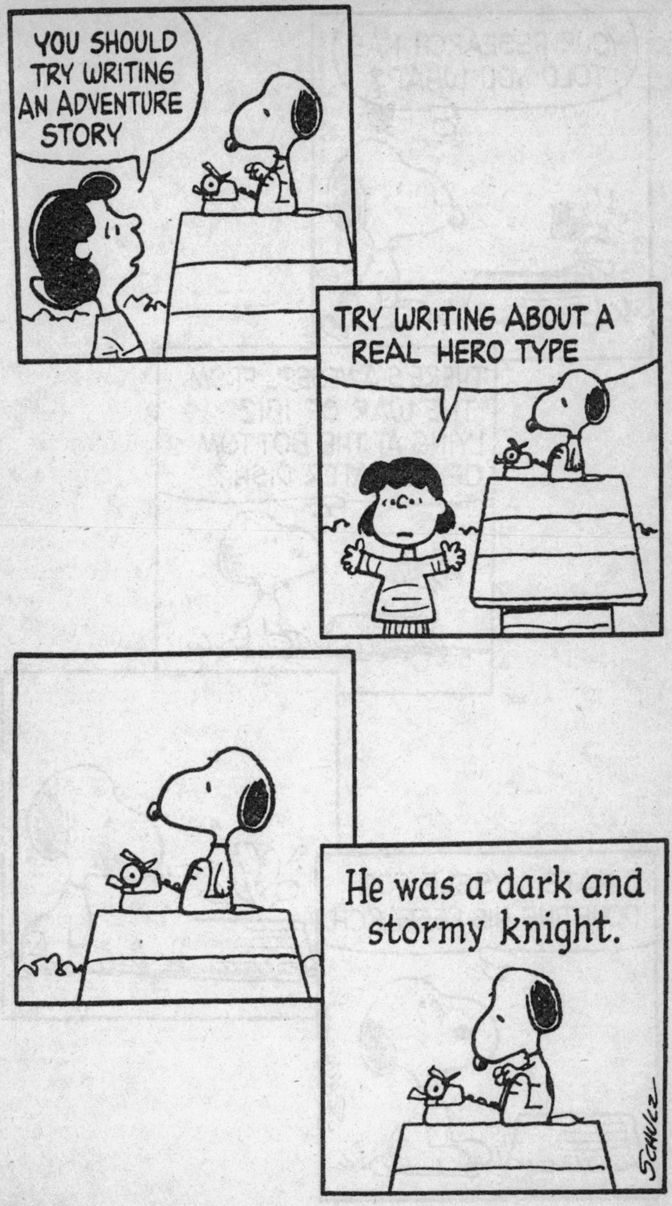
YOU SHOULD TRY WRITING AN ADVENTURE STORY
TRY WRITING ABOUT A REAL HERO TYPE
He was a dark and stormy knight.
SCHULZ

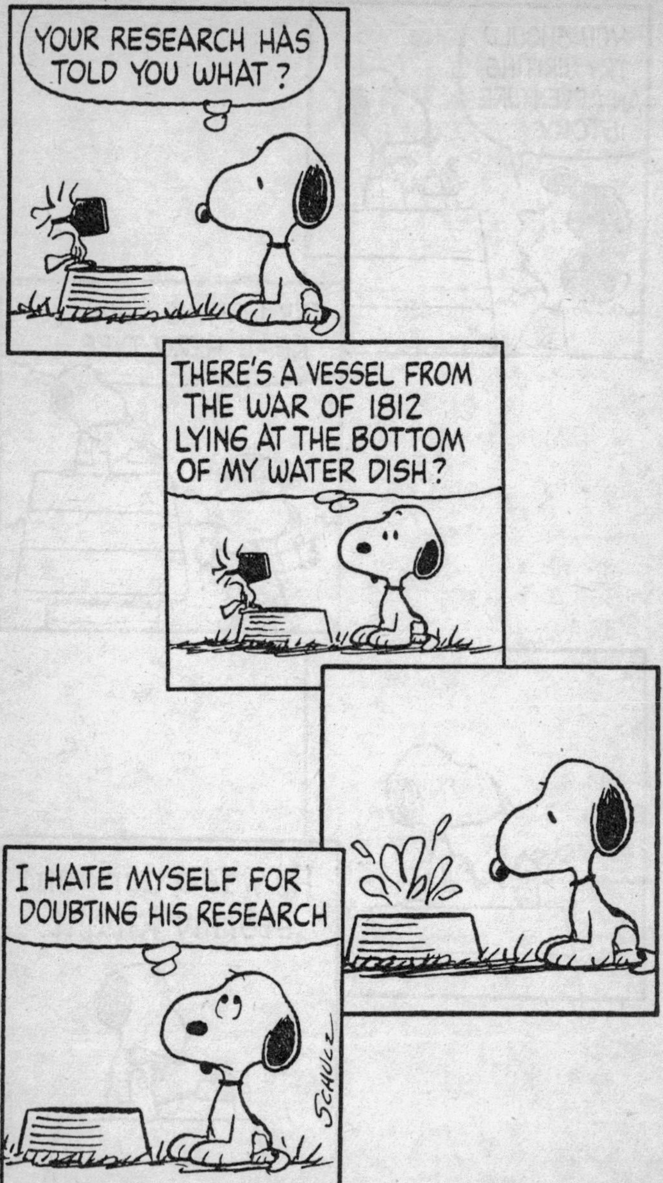
YOUR RESEARCH HAS TOLD YOU WHAT?
THERE'S A VESSEL FROM THE WAR OF 1812 LYING AT THE BOTTOM OF MY WATER DISH?
I HATE MYSELF FOR DOUBTING HIS RESEARCH
SCHULZ

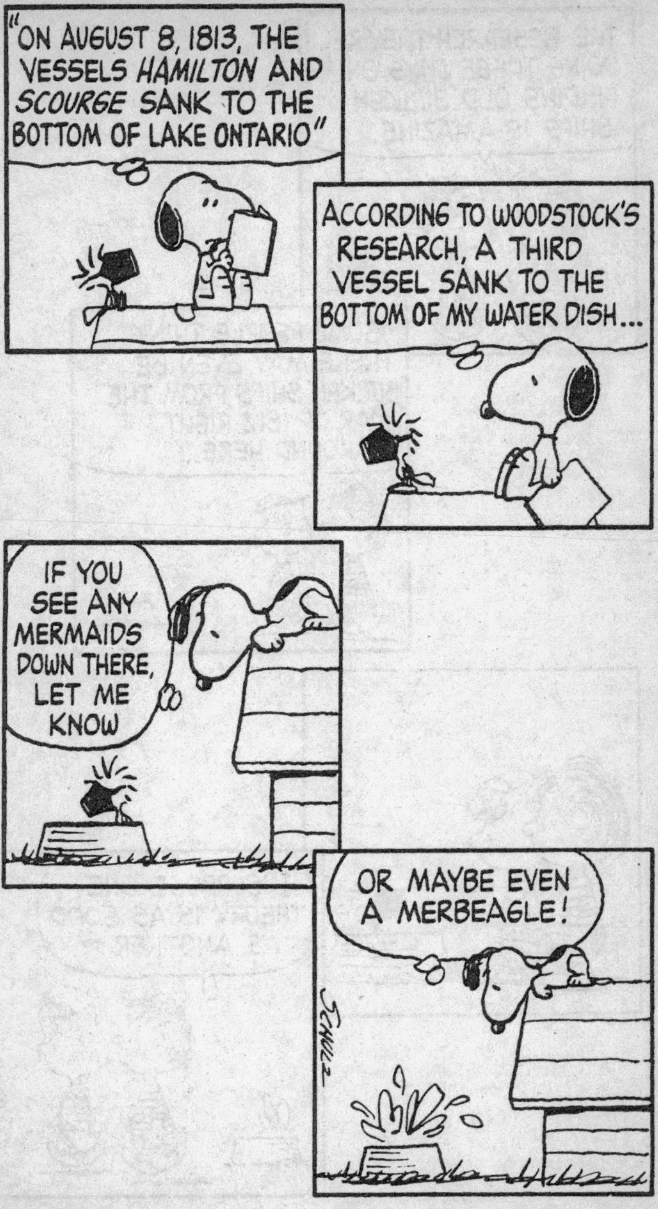
"ON AUGUST 8, 1813, THE VESSELS *HAMILTON* AND *SCOURGE* SANK TO THE BOTTOM OF LAKE ONTARIO"
ACCORDING TO WOODSTOCK'S RESEARCH, A THIRD VESSEL SANK TO THE BOTTOM OF MY WATER DISH...
IF YOU SEE ANY MERMAIDS DOWN THERE, LET ME KNOW
OR MAYBE EVEN A MERBEAGLE!
SCHULZ

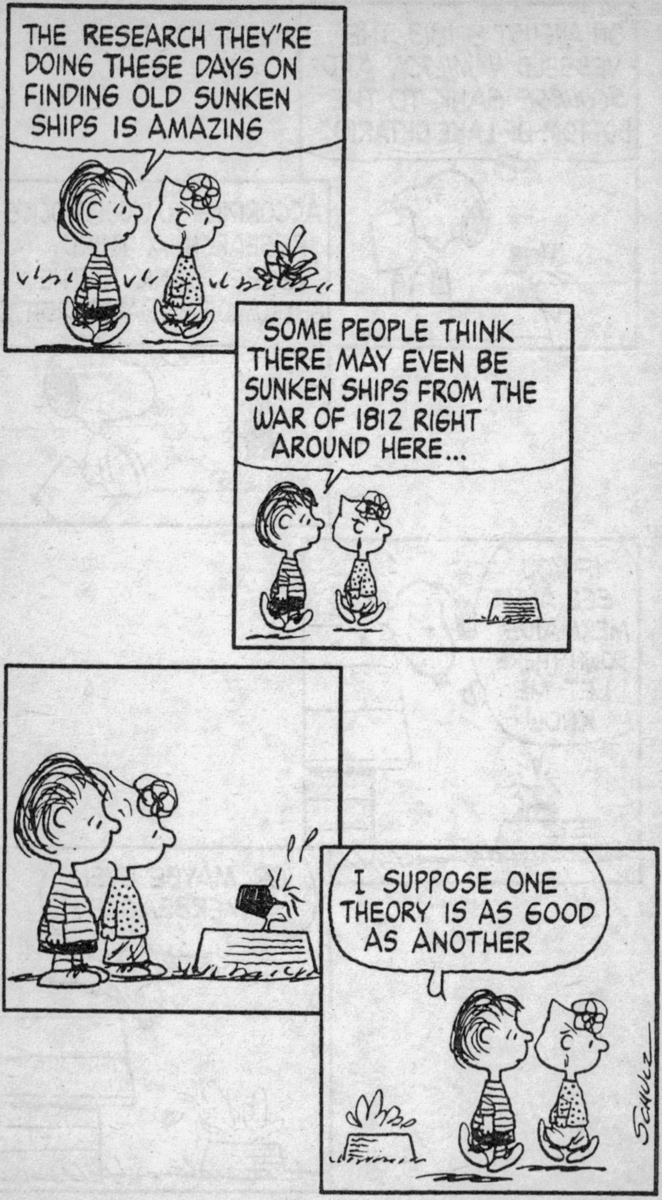
THE RESEARCH THEY'RE DOING THESE DAYS ON FINDING OLD SUNKEN SHIPS IS AMAZING
SOME PEOPLE THINK THERE MAY EVEN BE SUNKEN SHIPS FROM THE WAR OF 1812 RIGHT AROUND HERE...
I SUPPOSE ONE THEORY IS AS GOOD AS ANOTHER
SCHULZ

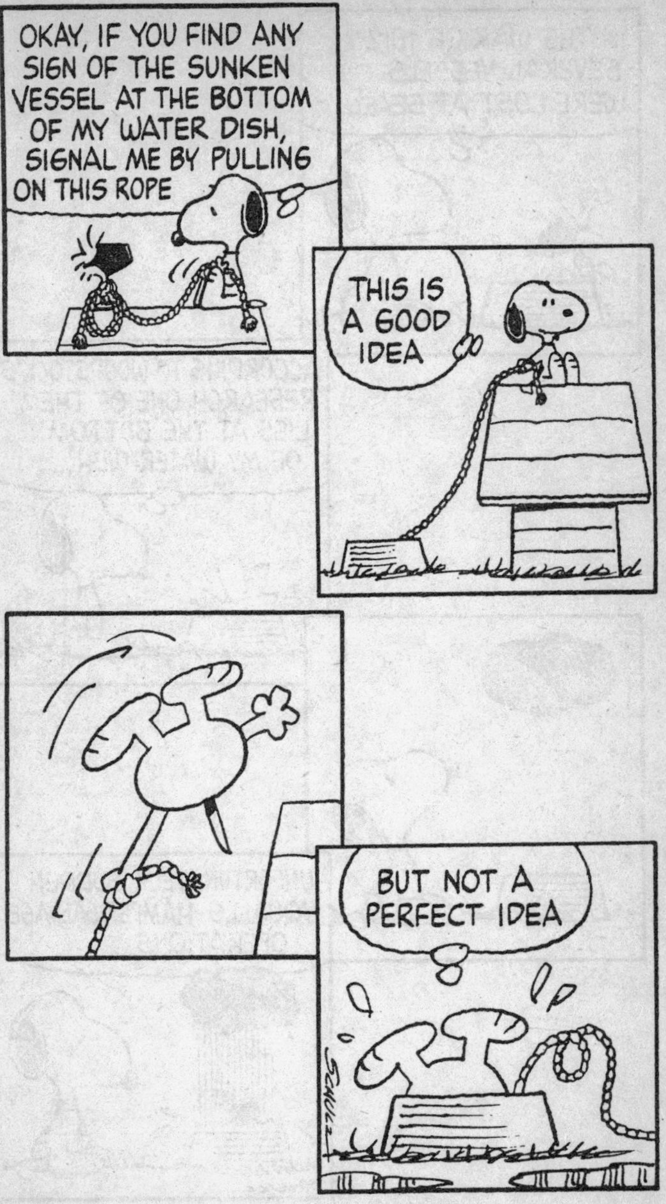
OKAY, IF YOU FIND ANY SIGN OF THE SUNKEN VESSEL AT THE BOTTOM OF MY WATER DISH, SIGNAL ME BY PULLING ON THIS ROPE
THIS IS A GOOD IDEA
BUT NOT A PERFECT IDEA
SCHULZ

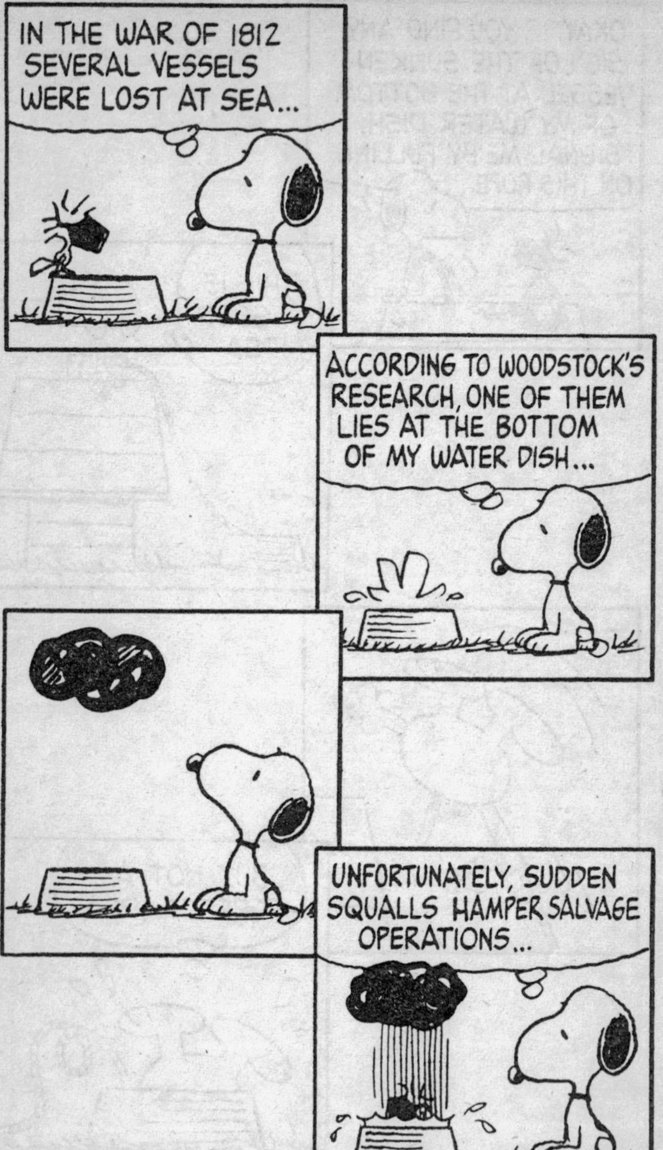
IN THE WAR OF 1812 SEVERAL VESSELS WERE LOST AT SEA...
ACCORDING TO WOODSTOCK'S RESEARCH, ONE OF THEM LIES AT THE BOTTOM OF MY WATER DISH...
UNFORTUNATELY, SUDDEN SQUALLS HAMPER SALVAGE OPERATIONS...
SCHULZ

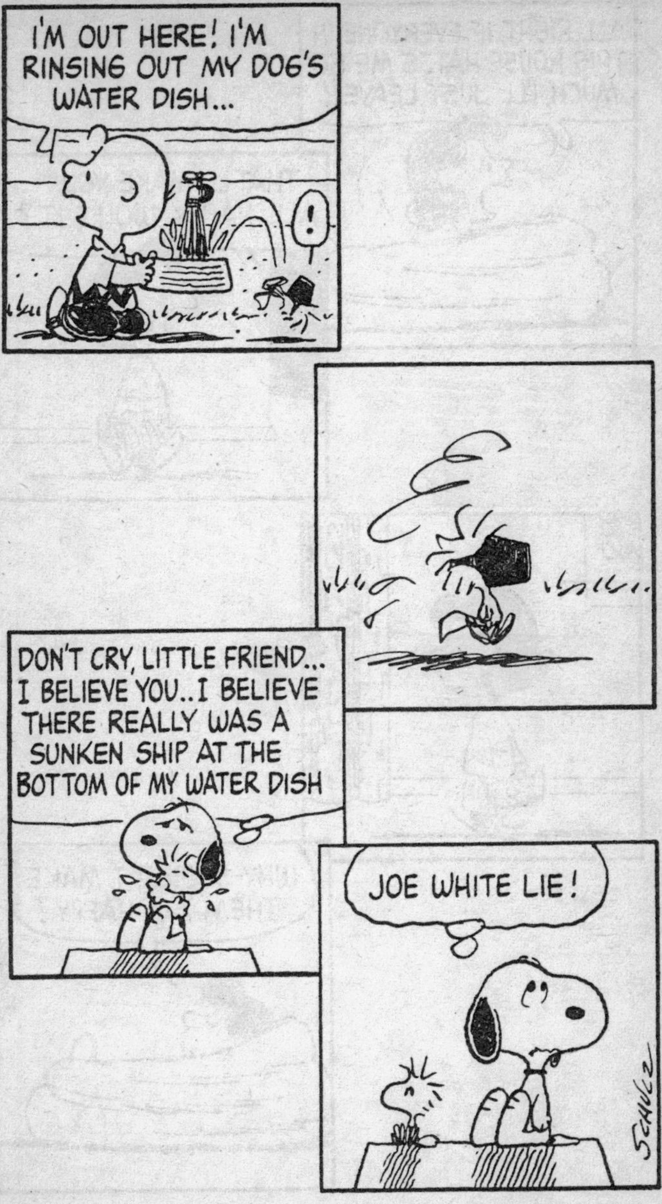
I'M OUT HERE! I'M RINSING OUT MY DOG'S WATER DISH...
!
DON'T CRY, LITTLE FRIEND... I BELIEVE YOU..I BELIEVE THERE REALLY WAS A SUNKEN SHIP AT THE BOTTOM OF MY WATER DISH
JOE WHITE LIE!
SCHULZ

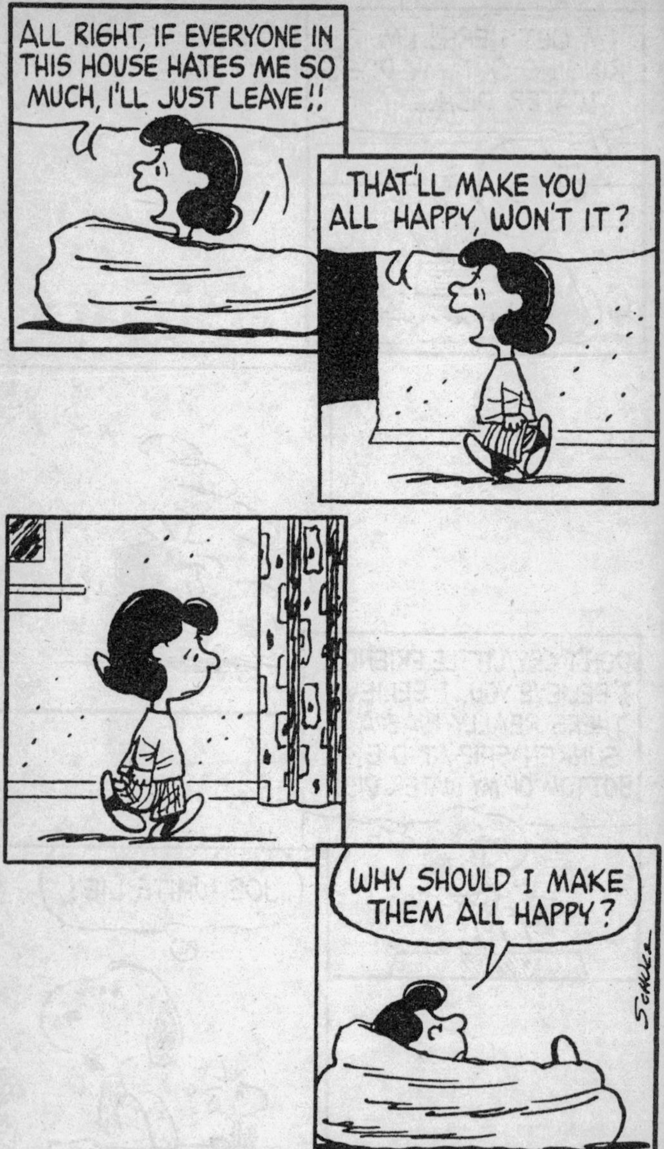

ALL RIGHT, IF EVERYONE IN THIS HOUSE HATES ME SO MUCH, I'LL JUST LEAVE!!
THAT'LL MAKE YOU ALL HAPPY, WON'T IT?
WHY SHOULD I MAKE THEM ALL HAPPY?
SCHULZ

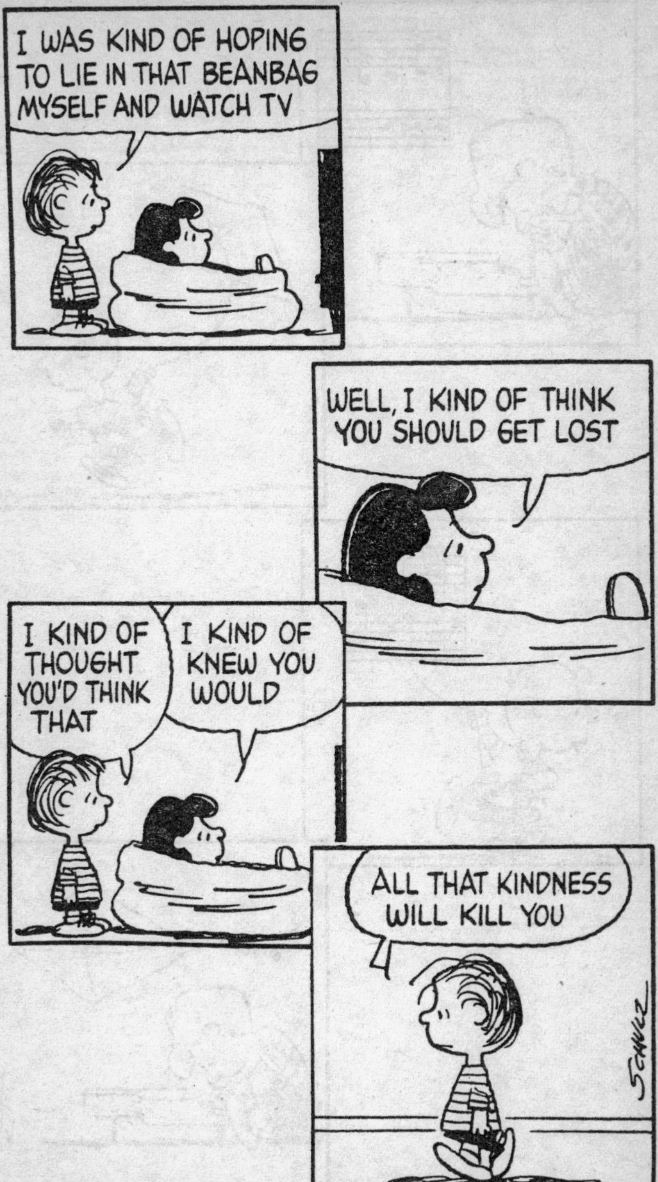
I WAS KIND OF HOPING TO LIE IN THAT BEANBAG MYSELF AND WATCH TV
WELL, I KIND OF THINK YOU SHOULD GET LOST
I KIND OF THOUGHT YOU'D THINK THAT
I KIND OF KNEW YOU WOULD
ALL THAT KINDNESS WILL KILL YOU
SCHULZ

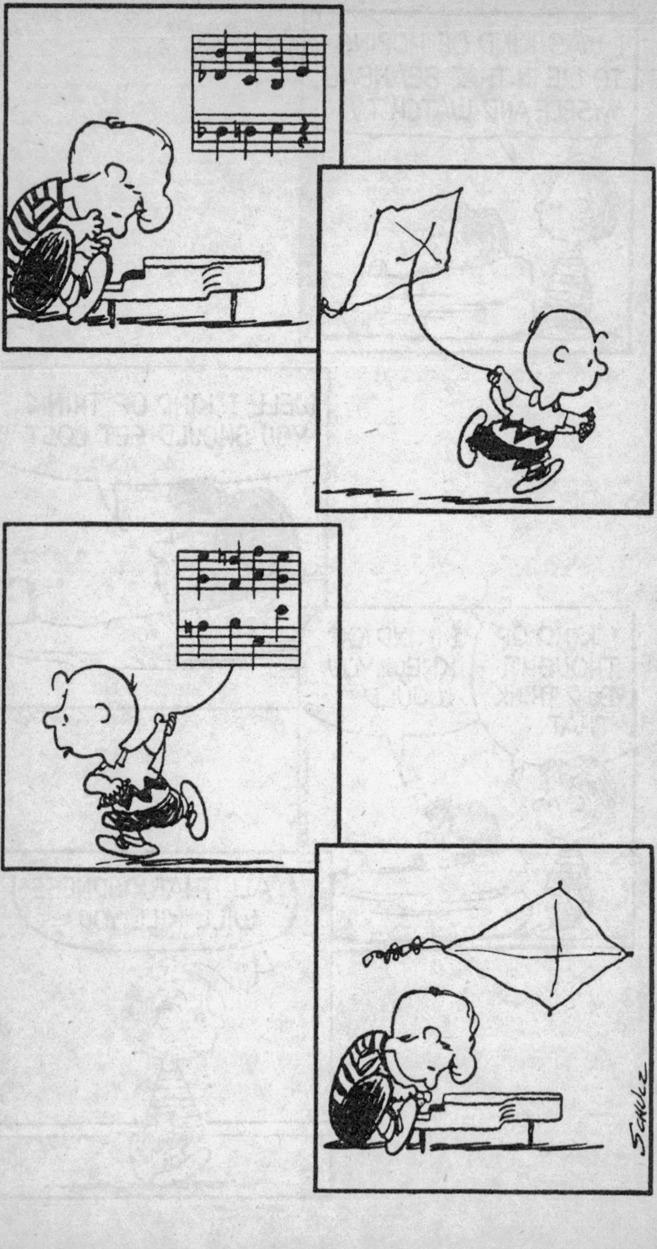

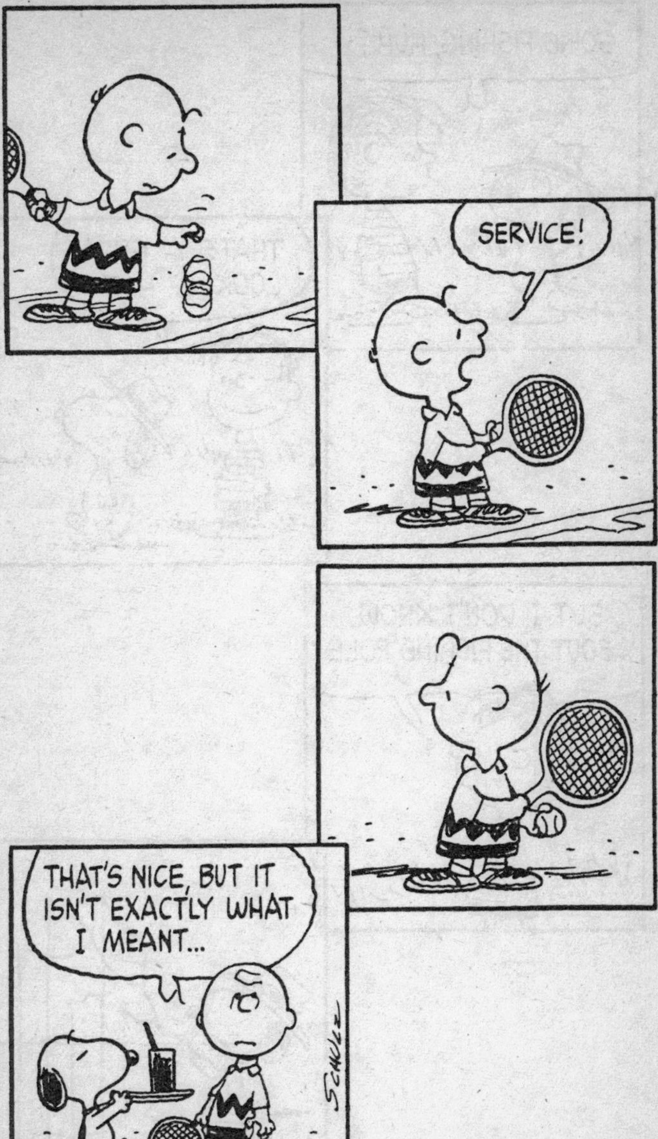
SERVICE!
THAT'S NICE, BUT IT ISN'T EXACTLY WHAT I MEANT...
SCHULZ

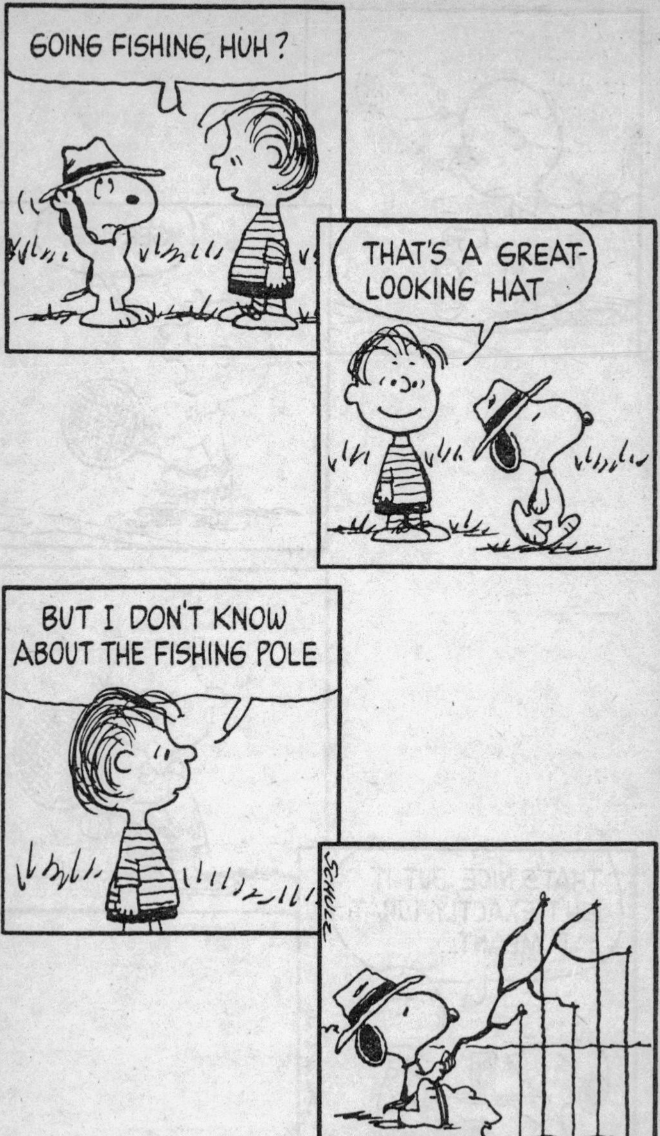
GOING FISHING, HUH?
THAT'S A GREAT-LOOKING HAT
BUT I DON'T KNOW ABOUT THE FISHING POLE
SCHULZ

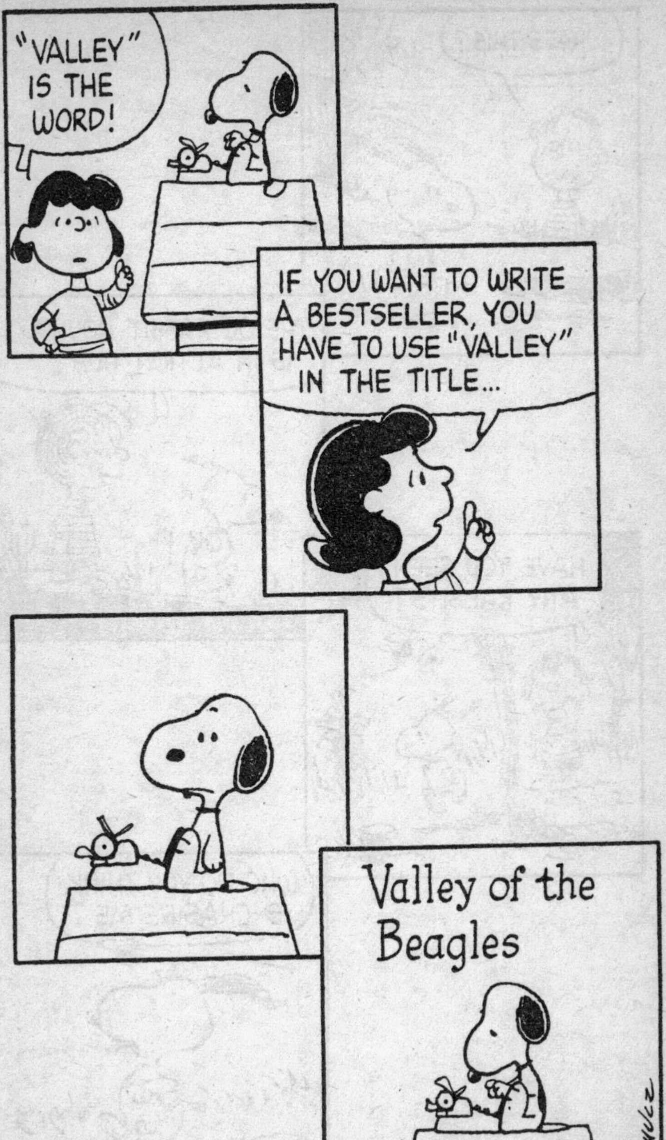
"VALLEY" IS THE WORD!
IF YOU WANT TO WRITE A BESTSELLER, YOU HAVE TO USE "VALLEY" IN THE TITLE...
Valley of the Beagles
SCHULZ

WHAT'S THIS ?
THE OL' RABBIT HOUND IS IN ACTION, HUH ?
HAVE YOU SEEN ANY RABBITS ?
WHO DO YOU THINK IS CHASING ME ?
SCHULZ

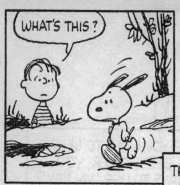

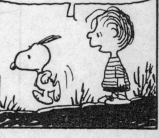

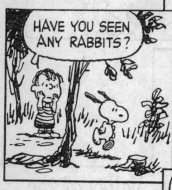

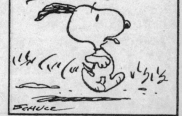

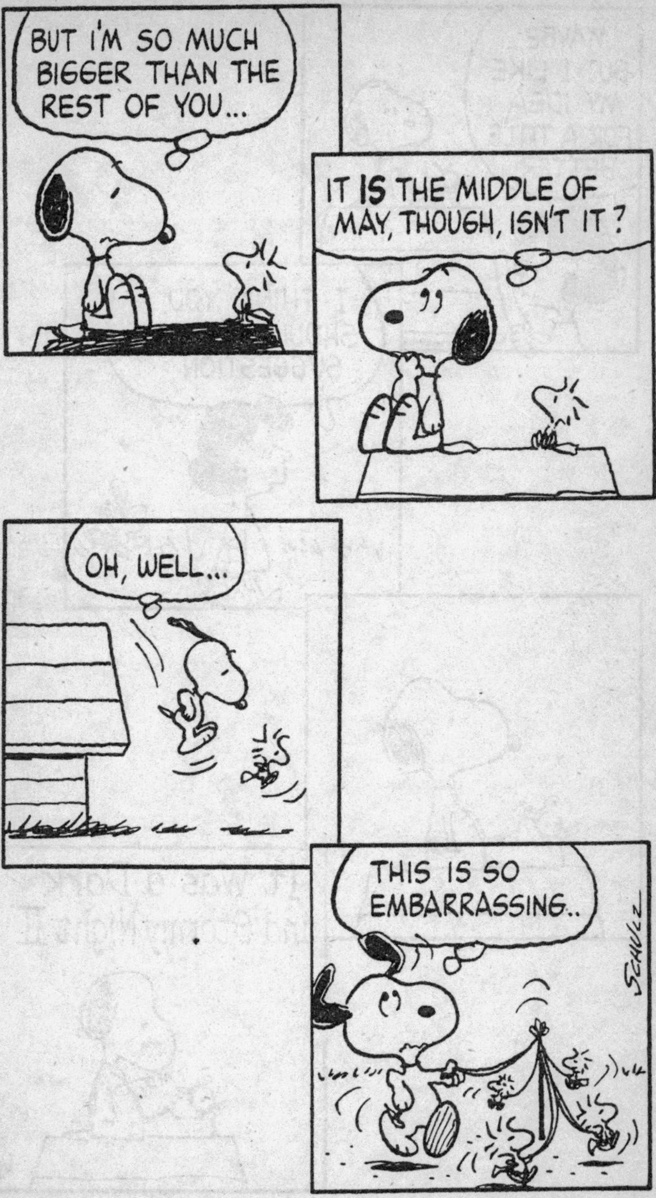
BUT I'M SO MUCH BIGGER THAN THE REST OF YOU...
IT IS THE MIDDLE OF MAY, THOUGH, ISN'T IT?
OH, WELL...
THIS IS SO EMBARRASSING..
SCHULZ

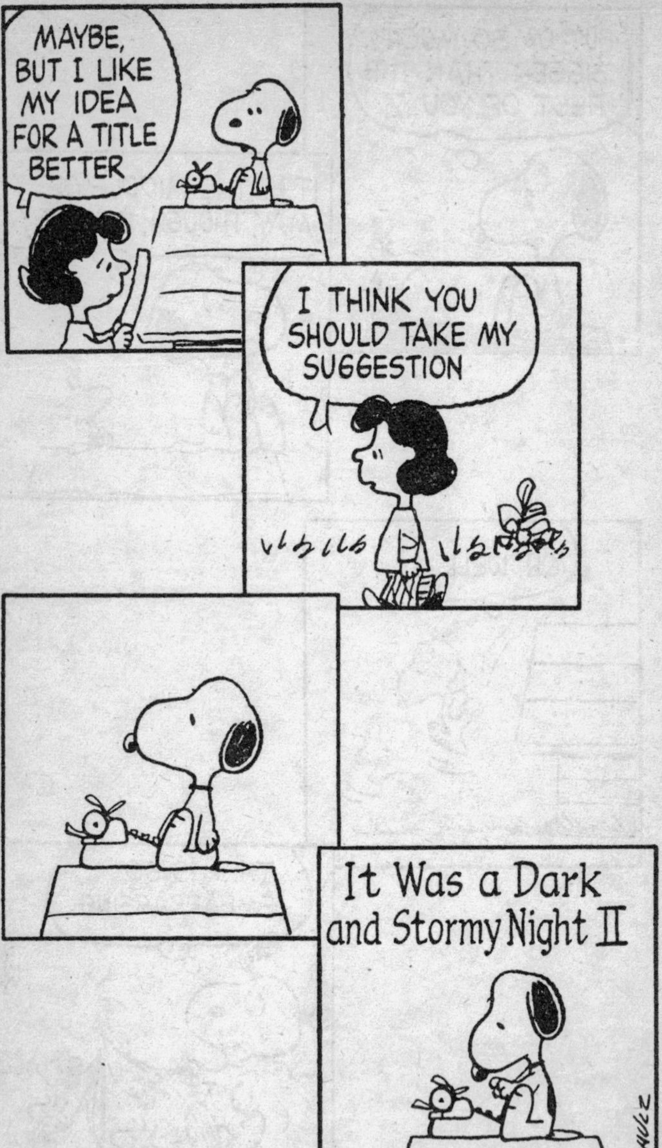
MAYBE, BUT I LIKE MY IDEA FOR A TITLE BETTER
I THINK YOU SHOULD TAKE MY SUGGESTION
It Was a Dark and Stormy Night II
SCHULZ

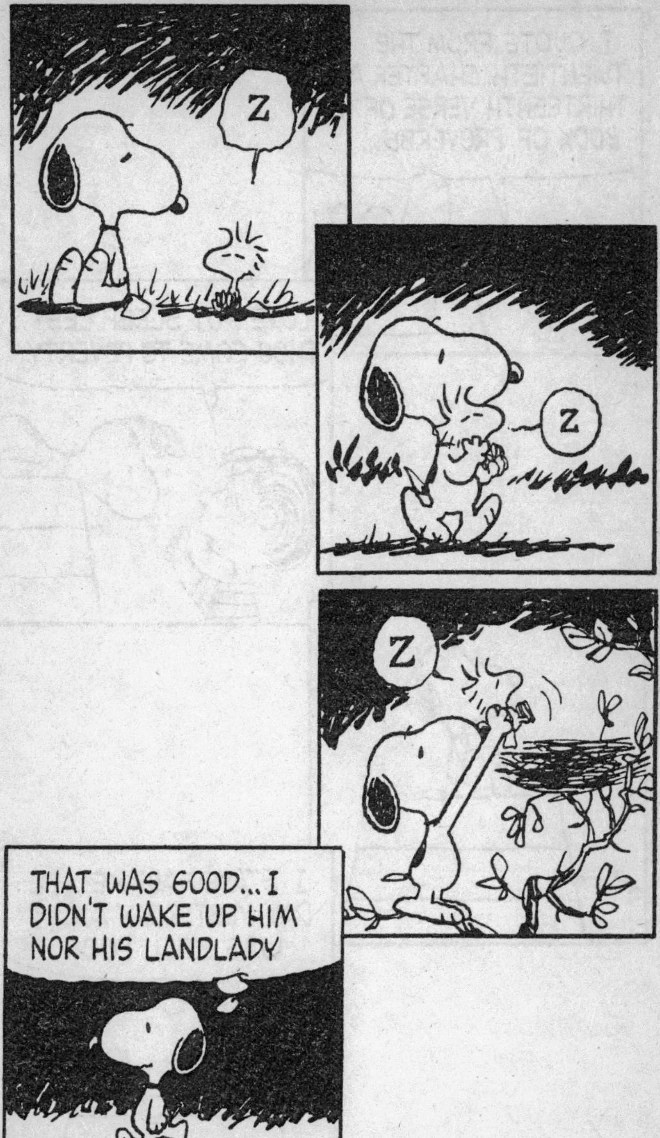
Z
Z
Z
THAT WAS GOOD... I DIDN'T WAKE UP HIM NOR HIS LANDLADY
SCHULZ

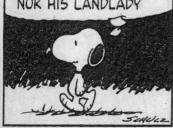

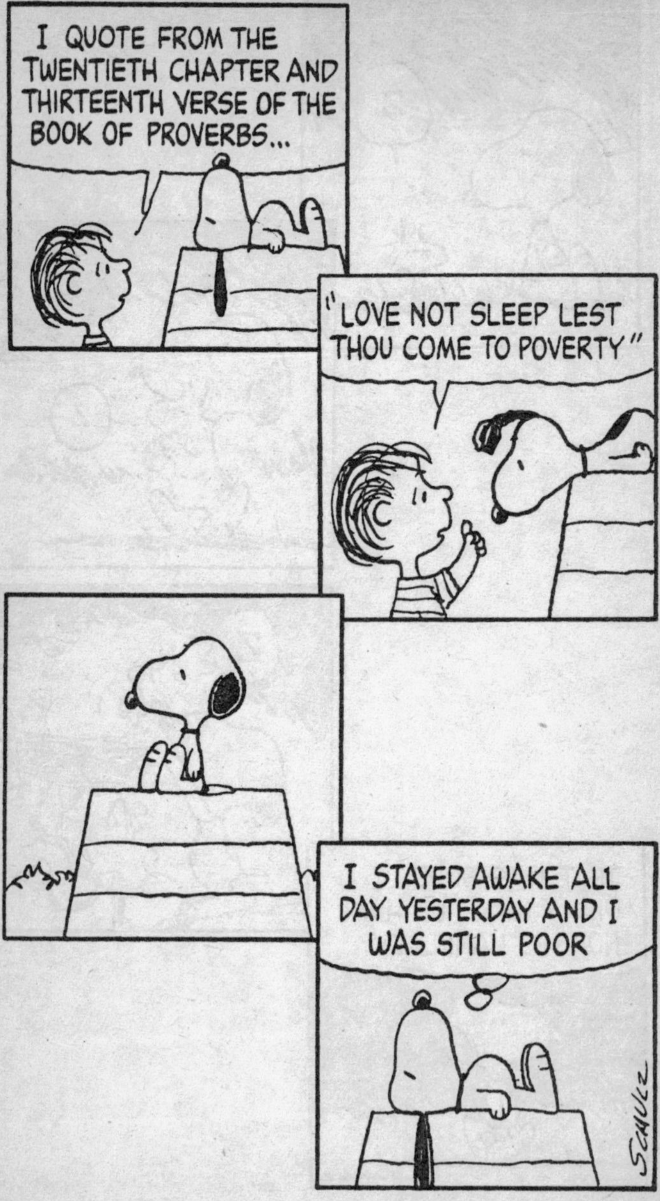
I QUOTE FROM THE TWENTIETH CHAPTER AND THIRTEENTH VERSE OF THE BOOK OF PROVERBS...
"LOVE NOT SLEEP LEST THOU COME TO POVERTY"
I STAYED AWAKE ALL DAY YESTERDAY AND I WAS STILL POOR
SCHULZ

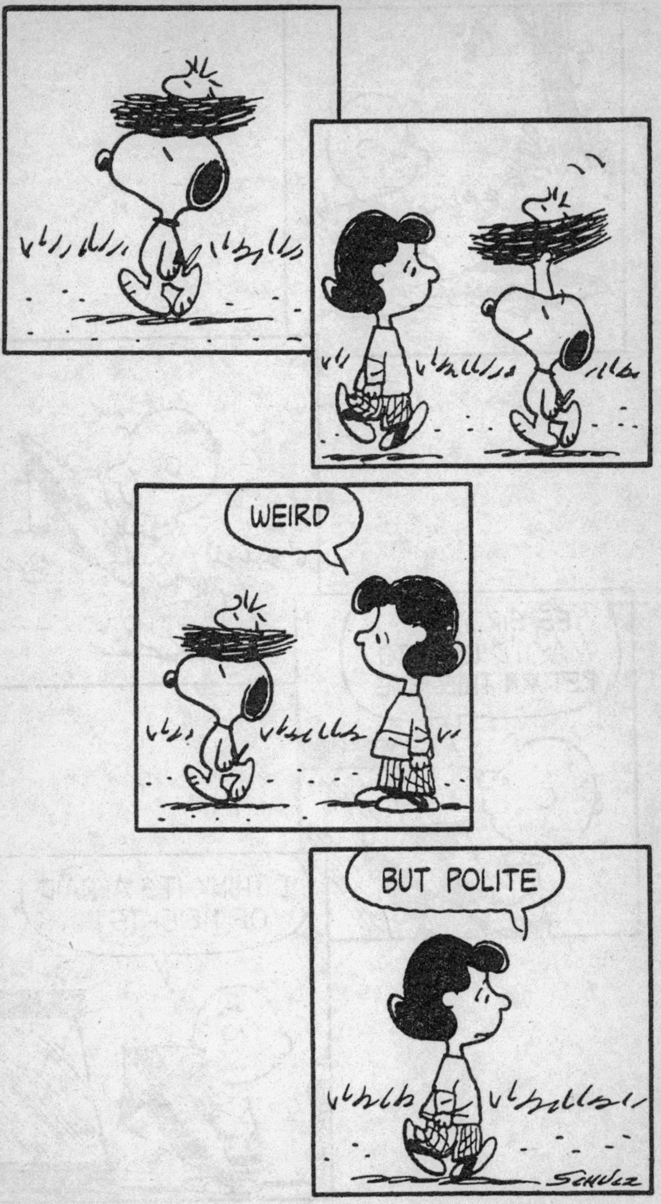
WEIRD
BUT POLITE
SCHULZ

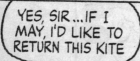

YES, SIR...IF I MAY, I'D LIKE TO RETURN THIS KITE

I THINK IT'S AFRAID OF HEIGHTS!

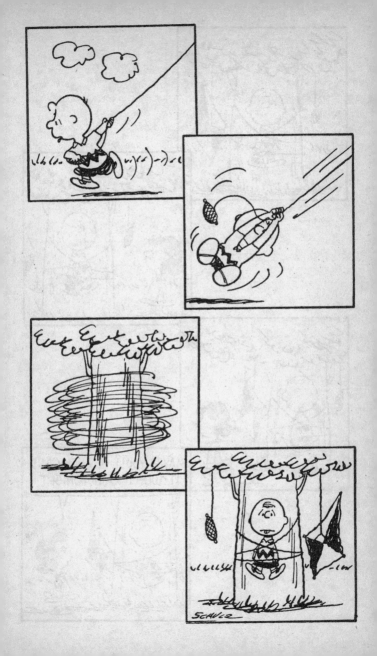

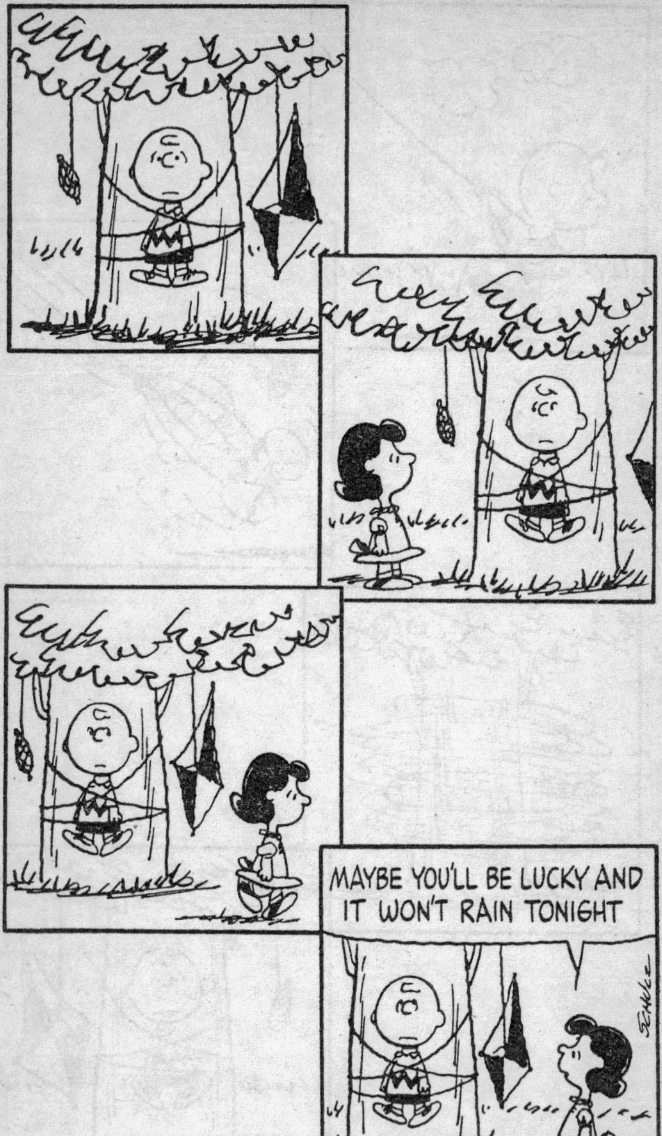
MAYBE YOU'LL BE LUCKY AND IT WON'T RAIN TONIGHT
SCHULZ

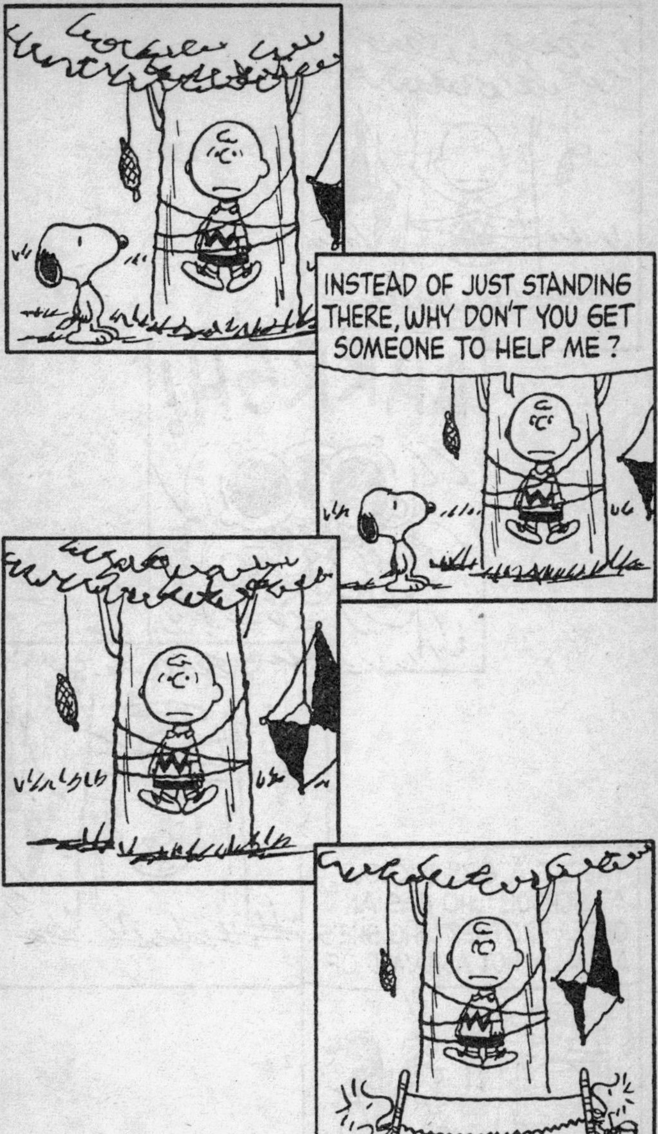
INSTEAD OF JUST STANDING THERE, WHY DON'T YOU GET SOMEONE TO HELP ME?
SCHULZ

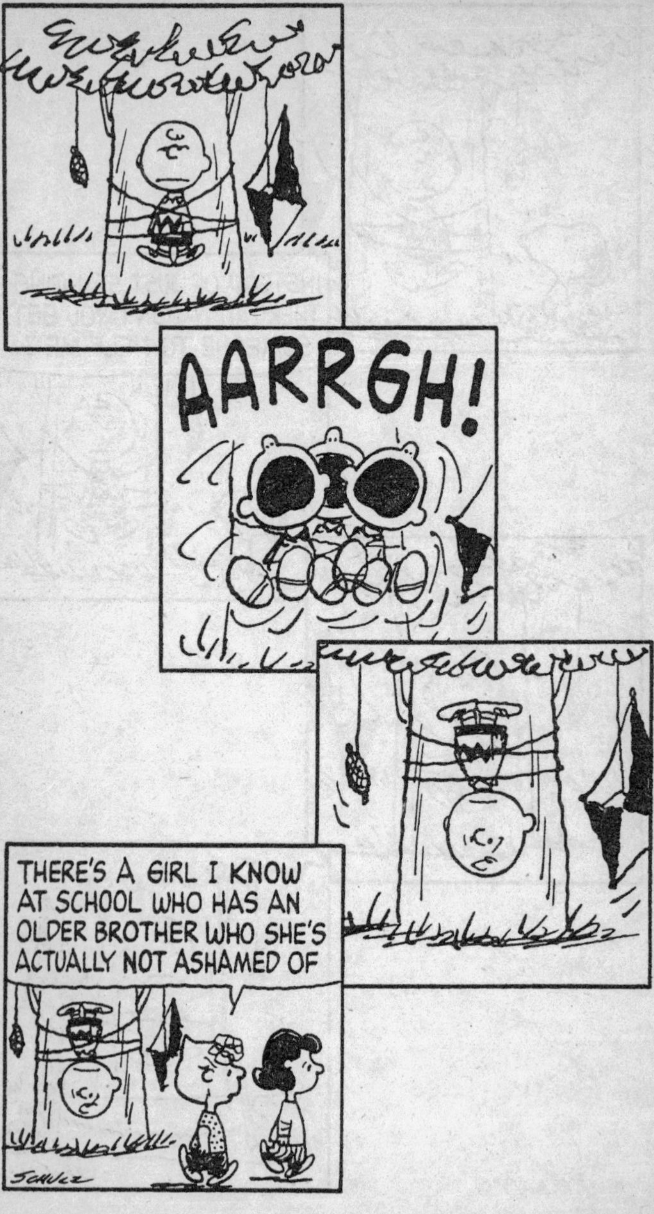
AARRGH!
THERE'S A GIRL I KNOW AT SCHOOL WHO HAS AN OLDER BROTHER WHO SHE'S ACTUALLY NOT ASHAMED OF
SCHULZ

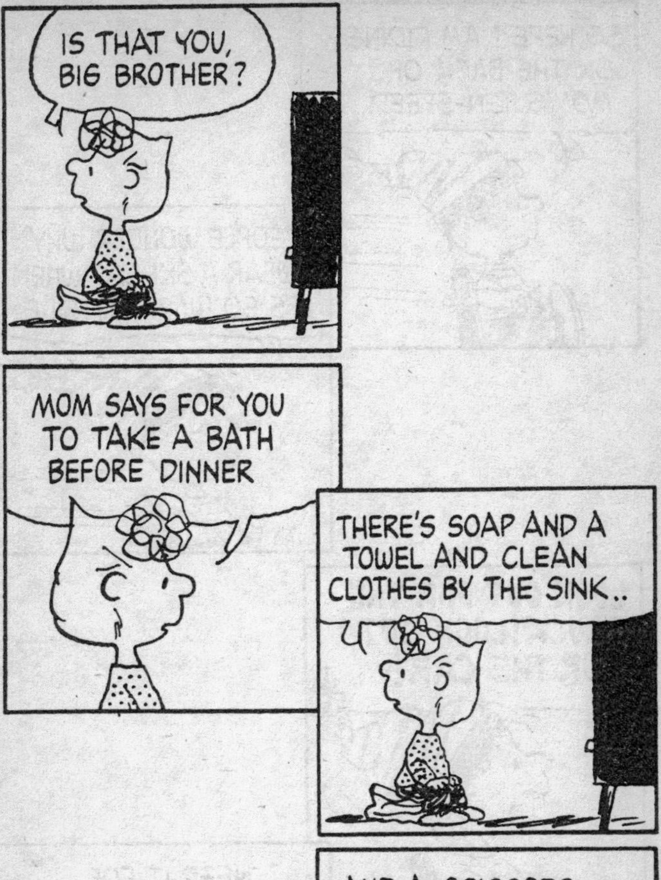
IS THAT YOU, BIG BROTHER?
MOM SAYS FOR YOU TO TAKE A BATH BEFORE DINNER
THERE'S SOAP AND A TOWEL AND CLEAN CLOTHES BY THE SINK..
AND A SCISSORS...
SCHULZ

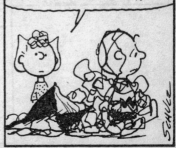

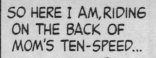
SO HERE I AM, RIDING ON THE BACK OF MOM'S TEN-SPEED...

PEOPLE WONDER WHY I WEAR A SKI CAP WHEN IT'S SO WARM OUTSIDE

LOOK OUT FOR THE TRUCK! LOOK OUT FOR THE CAR!

I NEED IT FOR GOING THROUGH TRAFFIC

SCHULZ

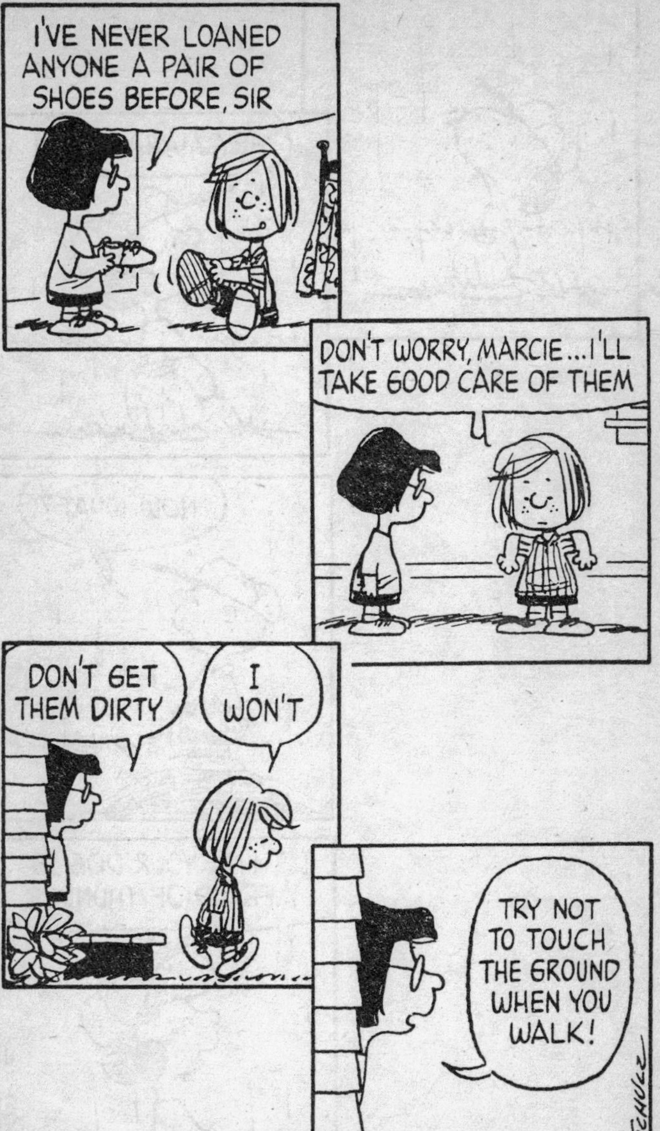
I'VE NEVER LOANED ANYONE A PAIR OF SHOES BEFORE, SIR
DON'T WORRY, MARCIE...I'LL TAKE GOOD CARE OF THEM
DON'T GET THEM DIRTY
I WON'T
TRY NOT TO TOUCH THE GROUND WHEN YOU WALK!
SCHULZ

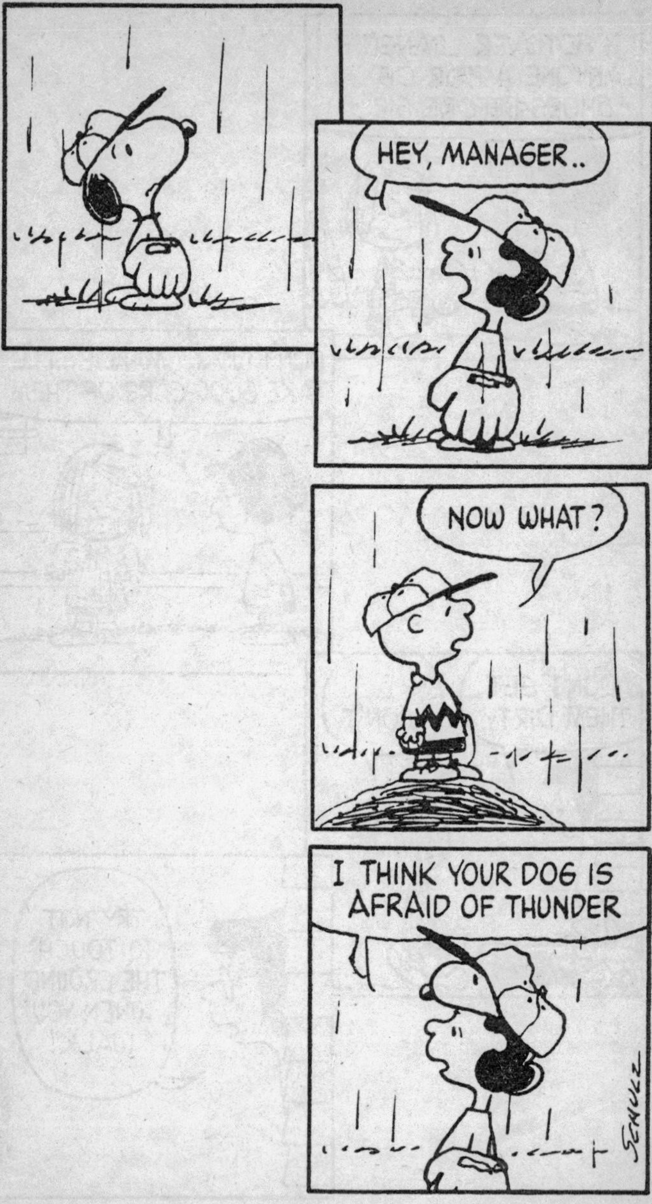
HEY, MANAGER..
NOW WHAT?
I THINK YOUR DOG IS AFRAID OF THUNDER
SCHULZ

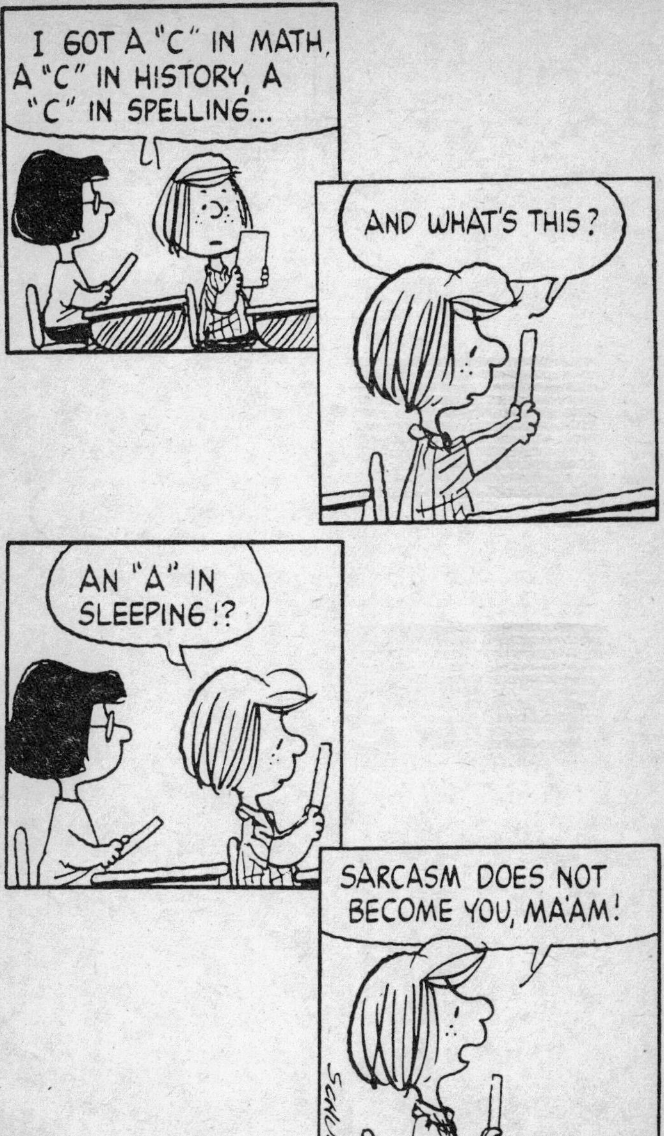
I GOT A "C" IN MATH, A "C" IN HISTORY, A "C" IN SPELLING...
AND WHAT'S THIS?
AN "A" IN SLEEPING!?
SARCASM DOES NOT BECOME YOU, MA'AM!